Living Judaism:
Talks, Poems and Articles

– DAVID TABOR –

Edited by Daniel Tabor and Michael Tabor

Foreword by Stefan C. Reif

An environmentally friendly book printed and bound in England by
www.printondemand-worldwide.com

Mixed Sources
Product group from well-managed
forests, and other controlled sources
www.fsc.org Cert no. TT-COC-002641
© 1996 Forest Stewardship Council

FSC

PEFC
PEFC/16-33-416

PEFC Certified
This product is
from sustainably
managed forests
and controlled
sources
www.pefc.org

This book is made entirely of chain-of-custody materials

www.fast-print.net/store.php

LIVING JUDAISM: TALKS, POEMS AND ARTICLES
Copyright © David Tabor 2015

Edited by Daniel Tabor and Michael Tabor
Foreword by Stefan C. Reif

A catalogue record for this book is available from the British Library

ISBN 978-178456-128-4

First published 2015 by
FASTPRINT PUBLISHING
Peterborough, England.

Contents

Foreword

I warmly applaud this initiative to print some of the numerous addresses that David Tabor gave in the course of the many decades in which he was not only a distinguished and widely acclaimed scholar in the University of Cambridge but also a devoted, active and much-loved member of the Cambridge Jewish community.

My late wife, Shulie, and I knew David and Hanna very well for a period of over thirty years. We came to love and admire them both, though for rather different qualities. David characterized much of what was best in the traditional circles of Anglo-Jewry. He was wholly devoted to a warm, vibrant but modern Judaism; to the Hebrew language in its spoken as well as its literary form; to Yiddish as his people's erstwhile *Mammaloshen*; and to Zionism and the State of Israel. At the same time, he never imposed his ideas on others, nor did he ever raise his voice in anger at those who might disagree with him. He regarded it as imperative to integrate the best ideas and practices of his family and his people with what he greatly valued in the democratic, liberal and educational values of the country that had given his family shelter from the anti-Semitism that it had experienced in Eastern Europe.

Although he was in many senses a traditionalist, David brought to bear on his traditions an inquisitive mind, a rational viewpoint and an awareness of the need to adjust to changing circumstances. I sat next to him in the Cambridge Synagogue in Thompson's Lane and he would often challenge me, gently and warmly, to explain why some religious practice or another had been retained when it sometimes appeared to him to make less sense than it might. We would discuss the matter for some time and, though clearly unconvinced by my explanations, he would not opt for a formal departure from the customs of his heritage.

When he came to my Talmud class, he also raised problems about some of the ancient rabbinic approaches to life and religion but never aggressively nor iconoclastically.

He discouraged divisiveness but encouraged sincere conviction. He thought carefully before making a point and hesitated to say anything that might give offence or cause pain. I remember only one occasion when he seemed to lose just a little of his total gentleness and calm. When a little girl came to sit on her father's knee in the synagogue, a visitor with rather narrow religious views, expressed his objections to the presence of a female among the men. David responded sharply but without raising his voice: "The idea that a three-year-old girl encourages inappropriate thoughts while one is praying seems to me in itself to be obscene."

On numerous occasions we hosted Hanna and David and were also made very welcome in their home. Our conversations would range over many topics but often related to Jewish history and contemporary events, Hebrew and Yiddish, and academic life. Hanna, for her part, was often a sharp foil to David's gentle parries. She represented what was best in the Jewish communities of Central Europe, excelling in literature and the arts, and never ceasing to maintain aspects of her sometime identity as a Jewish Berliner. Her home was immaculate, her catering a joy, and her presentation elegant in the utmost degree. She stated her mind in no uncertain terms and Shulie and I, who were well accustomed to both the Eastern and Central European traditions in our own families, adored her for it. Perhaps David loved her so much precisely because she represented, to a certain degree, an understanding of their people's thoughts and ways that was not identical to his own but somehow complemented it in a most appropriate fashion.

David and Hanna will live for ever in my heart and in the hearts of my family, as well as of their many Jewish and non-Jewish friends in Cambridge and beyond. With the printing of this booklet, those who did not have the privilege of enjoying David's company and his guidance will perhaps be inspired by what he once said and wrote.

Stefan C. Reif

Introduction

David Tabor (1913-2005) was the sixth of seven children, born in London to immigrant parents who came to Britain as refugees from Tsarist Russia in the first decade of the twentieth century. In the 1920s and '30s they settled in Notting Hill, and David and his siblings remembered a happy childhood in the small but vibrant Jewish community that existed there. David's father, formerly an armoury officer in the Imperial Russian army, supported the family through his business as a metalworker and craftsman, making customized fittings for customers. As the family became more established, the younger children in the Tabor family were able to pursue their education, keenly encouraged by their mother.

David studied Physics at Imperial College, and started his PhD there, though he soon transferred to Cambridge, where he spent the rest of his professional career. During World War II he went to Australia to conduct applied research that was dedicated to helping the Allied war effort, and it was there, through a shared interest in Zionist youth work, that he met Hannalene Stillschweig, a young refugee from Nazi Germany. They fell in love and got married, and in 1946 they returned to Cambridge, where David pursued a very successful career, receiving many honours over the following five decades in recognition of his work.

Alongside his professional success, David was deeply involved in the Cambridge Jewish community. He had a great love for the traditional Jewish liturgy, the Hebrew language and scriptures, and for Israel. For many years he gave the Kol Nidre addresses and Bar Mitzvah talks at the synagogue in Thompson's Lane, and he often officiated at funerals, giving the funeral oration (*hesped*). All his talks were drafted beforehand, and they were found among his papers after his death. It is these talks, with a minimum of editing, that are reproduced here, and apart from a couple of *hespedim*, they have not appeared in print before. We have also included a selection of David's poems and articles, as well as a couple of talks given on other occasions; most, though not all of them, have been published elsewhere.

For those who knew David, these talks will bring back many fond memories, and for those who did not know him, they will convey something of his depth of thought, fluency of expression and lightness of touch. Even after a gap of several decades, David still has something important to say to us about Judaism, Israel and our attempts – however imperfect – to lead a better life.

Daniel Tabor
Michael Tabor
September 2014

Kol Nidre talks:
1974-90

David Tabor

Erev Yom Kippur, September 1974

I t is customary on Kol Nidre night to make an appeal for Israel. It is right that we should do so. On the one hand this is perhaps the only occasion of the year when so many Jews of the most diverse backgrounds come together in a serious and solemn mood: on the other hand Israel is of pivotal interest to us all.

We need Israel. We need it as a home and a refuge for those Jews who are persecuted or, in other ways, cannot put up with the countries of their adoption. Those of us who have met Russian Jewish emigrants know how great is their need for a place of escape and a home where they can feel truly at home. We need Israel too because even in free countries of the West, Israel adds something to the dignity and pride of a Jew that he has not had for nearly 2,000 years. Israel is as tremendous psychological prop to the Jew of the Diaspora.

And Israel needs us. At this time last year, Israel, the Zionist movement and World Jewry were all living in that extraordinary illusory world that followed the 1967 Six Day War: the idea that, for ever, Israel could do virtually as it liked in the Middle East. Within a few days that illusion was shattered, perhaps for ever. And although in the end Israel achieved a remarkable military victory, something has changed that has shaken us to the roots. The military victory was achieved at great loss of life and limb – losses that can never be made good. It was also achieved at great material cost and this, at least, we can so something to help. Our financial support must be to help Israel - not with arms, but with the funds that make it possible for her to extend her social services, educational institutions and settlement of immigrants. But the Yom Kippur War of last year showed up something else: it showed that, apart from perhaps Holland, Israel has no friends in Europe – without American aid no-one knows how she would have managed. One thing became clear; when it comes to the crunch the only true friends of Israel are the Jewish people themselves. Our support of the United Israel Appeal is not only a matter of money – it is to reaffirm to ourselves and to assure our Israeli brothers that we are with them. The survival of Israel is as much our concern as theirs.

I hope you will all support the UIA as generously as you did last year to provide financial and moral support to the Israeli cause.

But Yom Kippur is not only an occasion for fund-raising, it was not decreed for that purpose. It is a religious festival which goes back a long, long way in the history of the Jews and in the history of Judaism. Indeed, of all the Jewish festivals it is the only one that has no national or agricultural associations. Unlike Passover (*Pesach*), Pentecost (*Shavuot*), Tabernacles (*Sukkot*), unlike Chanukah or Purim, unlike Rosh Hashanah, Yom Kippur has no secular equivalent. It is primarily a religious festival or it is nothing. And although religion is nowadays a bit unfashionable, something ought to be said about it.

Last week's *Jewish Chronicle* included an interview with a well-known Anglo-Jewish writer - a man of great sensitivity and intelligence, who confessed that he was a Jew only by the accident of birth – and I wondered about this. Because it seems to me that what he failed to realize is that there are a number of tremendous accidents – and I use the word in the old sense of a happening – that befell our people thousands of years ago which precondition the accident of his Jewish identity. The first was that great encounter between Abraham and God 3500 years ago when Abraham first expressed the vision of a moral monotheistic Lord, [the] Creator of the Universe. The second was that extraordinary confrontation between God and the Jewish people when, under Moses, God established a contract for all time with the Children of Israel. The third, five hundred years later was the unique phenomenon of the Hebrew prophets who, in language that moves us to this day, perceived on the one hand the special relationship between God and the Jews and the other, the universality of the Jewish God.

It is these tremendous events which set the stamp on the Jewish people for all time and created their identity as Jews: without these creative accidents, whoever our parents were, we would not be Jews.

Judaism has a long history and today many think of it as a relic of rituals and ceremonies. But behind these rituals and ceremonies lie, I suppose, fundamental views about Man, God and the Universe. Of these I would mention only one – that man is not only an animal, he is not simply another branch of the zoological tree, he carries within him some fragment of the divine spark. Of course, our daily struggle for existence, our animal nature, our ambitions and greed, our pride and our stubbornness, all these so encrust our personality that this poor spark is stifled and quenched. Indeed there are some people who go through their whole lives denying its existence or declaring that it is an illusion – like the deaf man who will deny that there is such a thing as music because he cannot hear it. It seems to me that Yom Kippur is very much concerned with this aspect of our spiritual personality.

The rabbis and saintly scholars who compiled the Yom Kippur service understood, and I am sure they are right, that it is when we confess our wrongdoings, when we are conscious of our failings, when we are aware of our greed, our pride, our indifference to others, when in fact we are in a contrite mood that we stand the best chance of breaking through this hardened worldly crust, that we stand the best chance of rekindling that divine spark that has [been] dormant in us for the whole year. And I think that our Yom Kippur service, its prayers, its melodies, its elegies, its call of the *shofar*, the fasting itself and the companionship of others in prayers around us are all part of this quest. Our religious thinkers, including Maimonides, recognized that our glimpse of the divine spark can never be sustained; it can never be more than fragmentary. But if we catch this glimpse even for a moment we can feel that this Yom Kippur has been fulfilled. May we all find fulfilment in this year's Yom Kippur service.

Erev Yom Kippur 5736
Evening of 14ᵗʰ September 1975

Yom Kippur is the most solemn day in the Jewish calendar. It has no secular equivalents. All our other festivals such as Passover, Pentecost and Tabernacles, have agricultural connections, the minor festivals of Purim and Hanukah have historical connections, [and] even Rosh Hashanah can be treated simply as the beginning of the calendar year. By contrast Yom Kippur has no such feature; it is purely a religious festival.

Nonetheless, it is customary on the eve of Yom Kippur to make an appeal for financial support for Israel - and this is right and proper. For this is the one occasion when Jews with the most varied backgrounds and interests come together – if not to assert their allegiance to the God of Israel – then at least to declare their loyalty to the House of Israel. And that is just what this appeal is about.

Earlier this year my wife and I visited Israel for the first time after many years and we were greatly impressed with so much of what we saw. Of the striking developments in agriculture, the continuous extension of new buildings and settlements, the enlargement of industry, of educational facilities, of research, the problems of the under-privileged communities, the difficulties of absorbing the new Russian immigrants. No doubt one could develop these themes into an emotional speech that would touch your hearts and open your pockets.

I would, however, prefer to talk about something else which made a great impression on me when we were in Jerusalem. I mentioned it to some friends here soon after our return from Israel and I think it appropriate for repetition on Erev Yom Kippur. It concerns prayer books – in fact two prayer books. The first was an edition published by the Israeli

Rabbinate. Naturally it is a prayer book entirely in Hebrew. What was striking about it was the fact that it had footnotes explaining archaic words in the prayers in terms of more familiar Hebrew words. Even more striking was the way in which Aramaic prayers were treated. As you may know, around 200 BCE the Jews stopped using Hebrew and began using Aramaic – or rather their own version of Aramaic. So widespread was this use that two of the prayers composed at that time by the Rabbis were deliberately written in Aramaic so that they could be more easily understood by the ordinary people – they were the *Kaddish* prayer of praise and the יקום פורקן [Aramaic: may the deliverance arise] prayer for grace and favour. In the prayer book I saw that the prayers were still printed in Aramaic, with a Hebrew translation. Clearly for Israelis, Hebrew was the language of easy comprehension – not Aramaic – and the wheel had turned full circle: in order to pray the Israelis are more at home in their ancient tongue.

The second book was a *siddur* [prayer book]. When I opened this I was amazed. It was a Hebrew prayer book with a Russian translation, photocopied from a Vilna edition published 80 years ago in the old Russian orthography with all those extra letters and signs which have now been abolished. And I thought: after the destruction of European and Eastern European Jewry by Hitler, and after sixty years of a policy of fervent assimilation by the Soviet authorities, who would have expected to see such a book anywhere other than in a museum? To see a new edition of this book was to witness a sort of resurrection, a תחית המתים [Hebrew: resurrection of the dead], that one would have never anticipated.

These two prayer books made me feel that in Israel not only had the Jews come home but Judaism had come home too – not to live in the interstices of a foreign culture but as a natural part of a full and flourishing Jewish life. And it is this connection between us – the House of Israel – and the Home of Israel that we need to strengthen to the maximum of our ability. We need Israel because it provides us with a sense of fulfilment, and achievement, and pride that we have lacked for two thousand years. They need us because they need to know that whatever other nations may promise we are their faithful and unfailing partners. The House of Israel and the Home of Israel is the partnership that we must sustain. I hope you will all give as generously as you possibly can to the UIA [United Israel Appeal].

And now I would like to say a few words about Yom Kippur itself. I ought to precede this by pointing out that I am a professing Jew, not a professional Jew and what I have to say has not got the authority of the London Beth Din, the Chief Rabbi's office, Dayan Swift, or even the Lubavitcher Rebbe.

I was much impressed by a book I recently read by E Bikermann which, amongst other things, referred to the Book of Jonah. As you know, this book is read tomorrow in the *minchah* [afternoon] service. The Rabbis held that there is luck in everything – even in the books of the Bible, and Jonah has the unique luck and distinction of being read in its entirety on the holiest day of the Jewish calendar.

We all know the story of the book: Jonah is instructed by God to warn the King and inhabitants of Nineveh – the great metropolis of the day – that because they are such sinners they will be destroyed in forty days. Jonah loathes the prospect and immediately jumps onto a ship travelling in the opposite direction. But God pursues him with a terrible storm. It is such a supernatural event that the sailors try to find out from one another who must be responsible. Jonah admits that he is a Hebrew fleeing from God's command and the sailors then make a most extraordinary public statement: Heaven should bear witness that they would never ordinarily throw a passenger into the sea, but if they don't their ship will sink and they will all be drowned. So they throw Jonah overboard, the storm subsides, the sailors are saved, and Jonah is swallowed by a whale which brings him to land and coughs him up onto the shore. Jonah realizes that there is no escape from God's command. He goes to Nineveh and traverses the city from end to end repeating God's warning. And then, quite unexpectedly, the King of Nineveh and his people truly repent of their evil ways and God decides to forgive and not destroy them. Poor Jonah is thoroughly fed-up: he feels that God has made a monkey of him and he retires in high dudgeon. And God then explains to him that He did not create men to destroy them – the wicked people have repented and they have therefore been saved from death.

The moral of the story is clear. The King of Nineveh did not have to throw away his idols, he did not have to adopt the God of Israel, he did not have to become an observant Jew: he had to repent of his evil ways and in that way he could be saved. There is an extraordinary sense of universalism in this story. Let us recall and contrast the attitude of a great religion like Christianity. Perhaps six hundred years after the Book of Jonah was written, at a time when it regarded itself as the newer religion of the future, Christianity stated *extra ecclesiam nulla salus*: outside the Church there is no salvation. And six hundred years after that another great world religion, Islam, which was to reconcile man with God for all mankind made a similar statement. The Book of Jonah represents a much more universal message.

And in case you should think that this is an accident, an unrepresentative view, consider the prayers which we shall recite tonight and tomorrow. They were composed by scholars and saints brought up in the great tradition of Rabbinic Judaism – where every facet of a man's life from the day he is born to the day he dies, from the moment he wakes up to the moment he goes to sleep is determined by rules and rituals deduced from the holy scriptures. Their *mitzvot* [Hebrew: commandments] control his life. Yet in the catalogue of sins which we confess and for which we ask forgiveness, our prayer book pays very little attention to our failure to fulfil the ritual requirements of the Law. Such ideas, of course, are not entirely absent – how could they be, seeing that the prayers have been written by Rabbinic Jews – but they are completely dominated by confessions of other sorts of sins. The vast majority are ethical or moral, and our prayers for forgiveness are for committing ethical or moral sins. I do not think that this is because the Rabbis took it for granted that we would all carry out all the *mitzvot*. It seems to me it is because they held the view that when it comes to the crunch, the issues on which we shall be judged, the issues which determine whether we shall be saved or not, are not ritual technicalities but more actions: and indeed for them the *mitzvot* themselves were not valued simply for their own sake but were intended to cultivate and strengthen our moral sensibilities. In this sense, Yom Kippur, the most Jewish of Jewish festivals, is also the most universal. The inclusion of the Book of Jonah is not a matter of luck – of chance – it is a very deliberate choice by the Rabbis. Our *machzor* [Hebrew: festival prayer book] repeats over and over again the message of Jonah – repent and you will be saved.

Of course, we must keep our sense of proportion. The Yom Kippur service is full of very particular, specifically Jewish themes, saturated with Jewish imagery, Jewish traditions, accounts of the Temple services, etc. Indeed, Judaism is full of tensions between the particular and [the] general, the tribal and the universal – the heart and the head.

I don't want to elaborate on this, and the last thing I want to do is to say a single word against the observance of the *mitzvot*. Heaven forbid! But the universalism of the Yom Kippur message is unmistakable.

Again, we must be clear about what is involved. The moral and ethical universalism that I have been talking about does not mean that Judaism is a form of International Boy Scouts association. It cannot even be identified with the Stoic ethics of Marcus Aurelius, however sublime and beautiful this may be. This universalism is based on a profound religious belief in God as the Creator, in the conviction that all of us contain a part of the divine spark that distinguishes us from animals. We belong to the animal kingdom – of this there is no doubt – but in addition a small part of us, if I may use the Hassidic phrase, belongs to the Kingdom of Heaven. And it is this part of our consciousness that Yom Kippur is about. It is concerned with rekindling the divine spark within us, neglected and choked as it is by the cares of the everyday world – so that we may more readily tune our actions to the moral and ethical values that monotheism and Judaism demand of us. The prayers, repeated over and over again, the tunes, the hymns, the *shofar* [Hebrew: musical instrument made from a ram's horn], the fasting, the feeling of communal worship, all these are to heighten the effect of this day, so that we may catch, if only for a second, a glimpse of this vision which is fundamental to Yom Kipper, and to the Judaism which we profess: that there is one God and we are His children: כי אנו בניך ואתה אלוהנו [Hebrew: For we are Your children and You are our God].

In the emotive language of the typically Jewish, typically universal prayer:

אבינו מלכנו חננו ועננו כי אין בנו מעשים.עשה עמנו צדקה
וחסד והושיענו.

[Hebrew: Our Father, Our King, be gracious to us and answer us, even though we have no good deeds; treat us with righteousness and kindness and save us.]

May we find this measure of fulfilment in the Yom Kippur service that we celebrate here together.

Kol Nidre Night
3ʳᵈ October 1976

I t is customary on Eve of Yom Kippur to appeal for support for Israel. It is right and proper that we should do so. For Israel occupies a unique place in the affections of the Jewish people – just as Yom Kippur occupies a unique place in the calendar of Judaism. Both lie at the heart of Jewish sentiment.

Some months ago we held a meeting in Cambridge to see what we could do to help Russian Jewish refuseniks. It soon became clear that the Soviet Union was not merely pursuing political anti-Zionism – but a policy involving all those hostile acts we have been hearing about for the last hundred years: *numerus clausus* at the University, exclusion from responsible position in the Government, in social institutions, in scientific institutions - and my thoughts went back to forty years ago when I was sitting at meetings in the Zionist offices in Great Russell Street, listening to the sad plight of German Jews. Of course, Soviet Jews don't have extermination camps but they are being subjected to enough forms of spiritual and physical harassment and degradation.

Two weeks ago my wife and I were on holiday in Jersey. One morning I spoke to a lady who had just bought a copy of a French newspaper. In my best French I asked what was the latest news from France. "The Croatian highjackers," she answered, "have just been sent back to New York." Then she looked at me closely. "Are you French?" she asked, "because you don't quite look English." "No," I replied, "I was born in England but I am a Jew." Then suddenly the floodgates opened. "I am French only by marriage," she said. "I am Yugoslavian. I am not Jewish but I lived in Zagreb during the war. What those Croatian nationalists did was appalling. They were vicious brutal murderers and they massacred all my Jewish friends. They made necklaces out of their eyeballs. They deserve the Electric Chair in New York – nothing less!"

Her vehemence was overwhelming. I wondered how the quiet peace of an English seaside resort could be so sheltered and invaded by this reminder of Jewish destiny.

I went back to my hotel and in *The Times* read of the growth of anti-Semitic literature in Argentina, initiated by Nazis supported by native anti-Semites and financed probably by Arab money. It seemed to me that so little has changed in our world situation. The Jewish universal word is not *shalom*, peace, but *gewold* – terror and violence and dismay. A hundred years ago it was in Yiddish, forty years ago in German – today in Russian, Croatian, Argentinian Spanish. Only one feature is different – the emergence and consolidation of the State of Israel. It provides a physical home for those who need it. We must help in order to help them. It provides a new-found sense of dignity to those Jews living in the free world - we must help Israel because thus we help ourselves.

Whether we agree in detail with Israel's government policy on this and that issue is beside the point. We need Israel no less than Israel needs us, both materially and psychologically. I hope that all of us will give as much as we can to Israel for our own sakes, for the sakes of those Jews who need refuge as well as for the sake of Israel itself.

Yom Kippur is the only Jewish festival which has no secular counterpart. It is a purely religious festival with tremendous emotional associations, that lasts far beyond today. For above all there is some sense of seriousness, of awe, which this day carries with it that is unique in our religious calendar. (I might even remark in a light-hearted way that Kol Nidre must be the only occasion in the whole year when Jews in synagogues actually stop talking to one another and that in itself is something very special.) We may come for a variety of reasons but for all of us this is a day with a special unique quality and flavour. It is a day of spiritual stocktaking in which we confess those sins of omission and commission, particularly in relation to our fellow men, that should help to clear our conscience and spur us on to better and nobler motives and actions in the year to come. For many of us it fulfils this role, at least to some extent.

But I would like to ask a very simple and fundamental and embarrassing question. In what way does this public confession of sins, this public confession of our moral failures, this public wailing and heart-beating differ from group therapy? In a very simple way it differs because God occupies a central place in the whole of the confessional liturgy. The Jews first got entangled with Abraham and we have never been able, not even our greatest *apikorsim* [i.e. those who negate the rabbinic tradition], to get him completely out of our hair. But it is not enough to feel that through Abraham we have automatically acquired a religious belief that validates the fundamentals of Judaism. Some orthodox Jews hold the view that this question of belief in God is of secondary importance. The main thing is to observe the commandments and the rituals. If you do that it doesn't matter too much what you believe or indeed if you believe anything at all. I don't know if this is true, but one thing I am sure of: it is less true of some occasions than others, and Yom Kippur must surely be one of the those occasions when it is legitimate to ask - if this service is not simply an elaborate form of group therapy – "Whom are we praying to?" After all, we shall be praying to God for a total of twelve hours; ought we not to spare a moment to ask what do we think of God in the scale of things, what part does God play in our prayers and in our view of the world, of reward and punishment, of evil, of suffering and all these terribly difficult problems?

I am sure you don't expect me to answer this for you in the next three minutes – it is a challenge for each one of us, though whether we shall find a satisfactory answer in three minutes, in three years or even in a lifetime, I don't know. As Maimonides pointed out, religious belief is not a sustained continuous state of heart and mind, but a fragmentary incomplete experience – or as the Hassidic rabbis would say in more picturesque language, "Only God sits secure on his stool – the rest of us are on very wobbly foundations." But the problem is real and it will not go away. In a similar context the rabbis said that although we may not be able to answer the problem with finality, neither are we free to desist from trying to answer it. And perhaps during this long service, when our concentration may wander, some small event or the recollections of a melody from another part of the service, may trigger off a response and maybe we shall be able to snatch, if only for a second, at that elusive faith on which the whole of our religion rests. For if we have this, all else will be added – if we do not have it, much else is lacking. I know that the Yom Kippur service itself offers one approach.

All religions with a strong tradition of ritual, and this is especially true of rabbinic Judaism, hold that it is in the atmosphere, in the ambience of the ritual that we are most likely to find the personal commitment to religious belief which makes the ritual itself acquire religious significance. And if we find this personal commitment, our personal belief latches in to the ritual: and the songs and the tunes, the prayers and the heart-beating, the opening and closing of the Ark, the standing up and the sitting down, the kneeling and the *shofar* blowing, all mount up to and into something more than an exercise in group therapy: a truly meaningful religious experience and the promise of spiritual renewal.

May we all be blessed with such a Yom Kippur this year.

Eve of Yom Kippur 1977

O nce again we have come together to celebrate Yom Kippur and it is customary on this evening to make an appeal for financial support for Israel. It seems to me that this is right and proper, not merely for the practical reasons that this is one of those rare occasions when so many Jews are gathered together, but because it is appropriate that on a day which lies at the heart of our religious commitment, we should pay tribute to the country which lies at the heart of our history and destiny as a people. It does not mean that we necessarily agree with every aspect of Israeli life or of governmental policy. It does mean that we are committed to the survival of Israel and to ensuring that it [will] flourish.

Israel presents two faces to the Jewish people. First it offers a home to those who need it. There is no sign as yet that anti-Semitism is about to disappear. Whole continents become infected with that persistent virus of discrimination, persecution or outlawry. The day before yesterday it was France, yesterday it was Germany, today it is the South American continent and in a different way the Soviet Union. Tomorrow it may be nearer. Indeed, in times of economic distress and acute unemployment, the position of Jews in this country would be far more uncomfortable if it were not for the coloured immigrants who carry the main brunt of intolerance. But that is one face of Israel – the home for those who need it.

It is also the one country where Jews do not live within the interstices of a dominant society and culture – the one country where for the first time in eighteen hundred years, Jews play a full and responsible part in every aspect of daily life, so that the Jew is totally involved as the creator of his own society and it is up to us to offer as much as we can to provide for her less privileged citizens. Our help is not only financial, it also demonstrates that we stand full-square behind Israel. For when it comes to the crunch, Israel's only sure ally is the Jewish people throughout the world. It is the partnership between the House of Israel and the Home of Israel to which we must dedicate our sustained support. I hope that you will all be as generous as possible in contributing to this year's UIA [United Israel Appeal].

It would be wrong of me not to say a few words about Yom Kippur itself, for after all it was not instituted solely as a means of raising funds for Israel. Yom Kippur is the only Jewish festival which has no historical or agricultural counterpart. It is wholly a religious festival in which we examine our consciences and ask ourselves if we could not do better next year.

Jews come to Yom Kippur service for many reasons. Some out of pure religious piety, some out of pure superstition, some out of a sense of identification with the House of Israel, if not with the God of Israel, some because it is the right thing to do and some because they feel the need to partake of the sort of group therapy that it provides. Whatever the motive, all those who come respond to the richness and emotional content of the ceremonial. The white *kittels* [Yiddish: a white robe that also serves as a burial shroud for male Jews] and the white covers of the *Sifrei Torah* [Hebrew: scrolls of the Pentateuch], the standing up, the sitting down, the opening of the Ark, the closing of the Ark, the beating of the breast, the kneeling and prostrating, the wailing and the chanting, the sad tunes and the jolly tunes, the blowing of the *shofar*, all these combine to move our hearts and emotions and also to provide continuity with last year's Yom Kippur as well as next year's.

The most explicit description of ritual and ceremonial is given in the portion of the *Torah* which we read tomorrow morning. It describes in detail the way in which Aaron was to be dressed, the scapegoat, the sacrifices, the procedures and activities of the priestly clan.

We have unfortunately no alternative sources to tell us how much of the ritual was in fact carried out in the wilderness to which this description applies. But we do have independent accounts of the Yom Kippur services as they were held a thousand years later in the time of the second temple. We have letters from a Greek Jew, Aristeas, describing the ceremony in Jerusalem for the benefit of Greek Jews living elsewhere - and an account by Marcus, a Roman Consul, written two hundred years later for the benefit of his friends in Rome. Both convey the richness and elaboration of the Yom Kippur ceremonial and the serious way it was regarded. Our own ceremonials are descended from these, though they cannot compare with them in pomp and majesty.

It therefore comes as an anticlimax, and I remember my son discussing this with me a couple of years ago, to read the *Haftorah* - the portion chosen by the rabbis from the other books of the Bible to supplement the portion from the *Torah*. This *Haftorah* comes from the Book of Isaiah, and was written at the time when the Temple ceremonial was being observed. What does it say?

Oh, House of Jacob, you complain we have fasted and God does not see we have afflicted our souls and God takes no cognisance. But God replies: "Oh House of Jacob, you fast for pleasure, believing that your voice will be heard on high. But is this the fast I ask for, to afflict our soul, to bow down your head, to spread sackcloth and ashes? Do you call this a fast – a day acceptable to the Lord? Behold the fast I have chosen is one in which you must loosen the bands of wickedness, undo the heavy burden, let the oppressed go free, feed the hungry, shelter the poor, clothe the naked.

"Then shall your light break forth as the morning. Then shall you call and the Lord shall answer."

In modern language what is Isaiah saying? This whole business of fasting, of moaning and breast-beating, of bowing and kneeling, this is not what God wants – this is not the way to win God's favour. What he wants is righteousness and justice, honesty, decency and compassion.

You may ask, how could the rabbis put this passage immediately after the whole ritual of the *Torah*? They were not imbeciles. They didn't have to read the English translation to know what they were saying. It would be an understatement to say that they knew Hebrew rather well. What is more, to the rabbis every word of the Bible was divinely inspired. How could they choose a *Haftorah* which so negates the preceding portion of the *Torah*?

The answer is clear and stares us in the face. The basic demand of Yom Kippur is a moral one. It is concerned with our moral behaviour to our fellow men. But moral principles fly in at one ear and out of the other, unless they are grounded in the deepest essence of our personality. As Solomon Schechter brilliantly remarked, Man does not live by oxygen alone. He needs all those motivations which come from the heart and the feelings.

It is this which the ritual and the ceremonies attempt to create: a response of our hearts and our emotions which provide the soil in which the moral principles can find sustenance and life. The ritual and the ceremonials are therefore essential but in themselves they are nothing. It is the moral imperatives of Judaism that justify them and give them their validity.

Let us hope that all of us will join wholeheartedly in the ceremonies of this day and plant, however small it may be, the seed of something better, more honest, and more compassionate in our natures for the year to come.

Eve of Yom Kippur
Tuesday, 10ᵗʰ October 1978

Once again we have come together to celebrate Yom Kippur and I rejoice to see this full and crowded synagogue – old friends and faces from Cambridge residents, new residents and visitors, students and academics. Welcome to you all. Especially may I express a welcome to new undergraduates – fresh persons – who celebrate their first Yom Kippur in Cambridge. I have a particularly weak spot for the students because I was once a student myself here before the war – the second - at a time when the Cambridge University Jewish society was first formed, and I was Secretary and Abba Evan was President. It was a time when this building had just been completed and was consecrated by Chief Rabbi Hertz. The atmosphere and spirit of the student services – in those days there were only half a dozen Jewish residents in Cambridge - made a deep impression on me and to this day I am moved by the informality, the sincerity and the sense of involvement and participation of all those who attend our services. I hope that all our Freshmen and Freshwomen will enter into the life of the community and the synagogue, and continue this marvellous tradition. And whilst I am talking of this I am sure that the new, larger synagogue that in due course will arise in this area will continue this marvellous tradition.

It is customary on this evening to make an appeal for financial support for Israel. It seems to me that this is right and proper, not merely because this is one of those rare occasions when so many Jews are gathered together, but because it is appropriate that on a day which lies at the heart of our religious commitment, we should demonstrate our support for the country which lies at the heart of our history and destiny as a people. This does not mean that we necessarily agree with every aspect of Israeli life or governmental policy. It does mean that we are committed to the survival of Israel and to ensuring that it flourish[es].

Israel presents two faces to the Jewish people. First it offers a house to those who need it. In the 1900s for Jews from Czarist Russia, in the 1920s and '30s for Jews from Poland, in 1930s and '40s for Jews from Germany, in 1940s and '50s for Jewish survivors of the Nazi death camps, in the 1950s and '60s for Jews from Arab countries, in 1960–1970 for Jews of South America, and since 1970 for Jews from Soviet Russia. And we do not have to think that this is a feature that affects the life of Jews somewhere else. In one form or another anti-Semitism shows no sign of diminishing, even if it sometimes clothes itself in other terms. Even in this country, in the present climate of inflation and unemployment, we should feel far less comfortable as Jews if it were not for the coloured immigrants who carry the main brunt of intolerance. That is one face of Israel – the home for those who need it.

It is also the one country where Jews do not live within the interstices of a dominant society and culture – where for the first time in eighteen hundred years Jews play a full and responsible part in every aspect of daily life. The Jew is the creator of his own society.

Today we see the first prospects of the outbreak of peace in the Middle East, and this means that our financial support to Israel can be concentrated on the social needs of the country and the problems of the disadvantaged sections of the community. We must provide Israel with financial support, not only because the money is needed, but because we must demonstrate our four-square support for Israel. For when it comes to the crunch, Israel's only sure ally is the Jewish people throughout the world. It is the partnership between the House of Israel and the Home of Israel to which we must dedicate our sustained support. I hope you will all be as generous as possible in contributing to this year's UIA.

But it would be wrong of me not to say a few words about Yom Kippur itself, for after all it was not instituted solely as a means of raising funds for Israel.

Yom Kippur is the most solemn religious festival in the Jewish calendar. In Orthodox communities throughout the world Jews will be gathered together to participate in the ancient ritual. In some there will be an impassioned address calling on us to repent, tugging at our hearts and emotions, tuning us in to the service which is to follow. I cannot do that but I would like to raise one simple point that is so obvious that we may lose sight of it. Let us ask ourselves what we are. Are we just a collection of chemicals – worth at the present rate of exchange about 85p? Are we simply a bundle of neuroses conditioned by our genes and our upbringing? Are we an assembly of reflexes which simply respond to the stimuli to which we are subjected? Are we just the products of our society and our material environment? To some extent we are all these but in addition there is one very small part of us that escapes these categories – it is that small part of us that constitutes our own personality and makes each of us, even in a very limited way, an individual in his own right. And it is this vital part of us which you may call the divine spark within us, which is crucial, for in our religious tradition it is capable of making moral choices. No other living creature, as far as we know, has the intellectual or spiritual capacity of making moral choices and the Yom Kippur service continuously aims at reminding us of this fact. And since in Judaism we do not believe in intermediaries between us and our God, it is for each of us as individuals to respond to the moral challenge – to recall our past failings and to assert that, with God's help, we will do better.

Our community is blessed with gifted and dedicated members who will conduct our traditional service in the traditional way so that we can respond to the richness and emotional content of the ceremonial. The white *kittels* and the white [covers for the] *Torah* scrolls, the standing up, the sitting down, the opening of the Ark, the closing of the Ark, the beating of the breast, the kneeling and the prostrating, the wailing and the chanting, the sad tunes and the jolly tunes, the blowing of the *shofar* - all these combine to move our hearts, our feelings and our minds. But the rest – the rest is up to each of us.

Let me conclude with a short prayer from our liturgy.

Lord of the Universe, fulfil the wishes of our hearts for good, yield our desire and grant our petition – pardon all our iniquities with loving kindness and mercy. Purify us from our sins, our iniquities and our transgressions, and remember us with a good remembrance. Grant us salvation and compassion and remember us for a long and good life, for peace, for sustenance and for support.

Eve of Yom Kippur
Tuesday, 30th September 1979

Once again we have come together to celebrate Yom Kippur and I rejoice to see this full and crowded synagogue – old friends and faces from Cambridge residents, new residents and visitors, a few students and academics. Welcome to you all. We hope that you will all share in the informality, the sincerity and the sense of involvement and participation that has always characterized our services here.

It is customary on this evening to make an appeal on behalf of Israel. It seems to me that this is right and proper – not only because this is one of those occasions when so many Jews are gathered together, but because it is appropriate that on a day which lies at the heart of our religious commitment we should demonstrate our support for the country which lies at the heart of our history and destiny as a people. But this year I would like to approach it a little differently.

I have recently been reading a two-volume work on Jewish letters throughout the ages – the first is a letter from King Solomon to Hiram, King of Tyre, asking for skilled labourers to help build the Temple – the last letter is from the beginning of the Emancipation two hundred years ago. This marvellous pen picture from the life and times of Jews throughout the ages reveals a number of constant themes – unchanging, however much the situations may seem to differ. I cannot deal with them all, but one, which is specially prominent, is also specially relevant – the common destiny of the Jews – their inescapable destiny. Individuals may opt out, and indeed have done so since the Jews came into existence, but collectively we are tied to an experience that challenges us over and over again. It is the problem of the Jew finding a place within the economy where he can make a decent living, provide a decent religious and secular education for his children, and live in safety and security without fear or discrimination. Because of this recurrent theme of uncertainty, instability, persecution and physical danger the Jews have developed a wonderful tradition of self-help. As the rabbis say, all Jews are connected to one another.

The story of Jewish suffering, of the Jew being the whipping boy for all kinds of social, economic and military failures of the host nation began during the first dispersion in Persia two thousand years ago, and has continued since. In the book I have referred to, the last great cataclysm which devastated European Jewry was the uprising of Chmielnicki nearly three hundred and fifty years ago. This Ukrainian patriot attempted to overthrow the rule of the Polish nobility, and in the process massacred an enormous part of central and eastern European Jewry. The Chmielnicki pogroms not only led to an estimate of over 100,000 deaths...it fragmented and disrupted Jewish communal life, it undermined Jewish confidence and it turned Eastern Jewry in on itself. Its influence has left its mark on Jewish thought and the Jewish *Weltanschaung* to this very day.

But three hundred and fifty years ago is a long time and we all have short memories. Our memories are limited by our lifespan. We might remember what our parents or grandparents remember, but more distant periods seem unreal and part of bookish history, not real day-to-day events.

But my friends, less than thirty-five years ago an event took place which puts Chmielnicki into the shade. The final solution of European Jewry by Hitler is something that has occurred in our own lifetime or in the lifetime of our parents. It affects all Jews, rich Jews, poor Jews, old and young Jews, Jewish men, Jewish women, adults and children, orthodox and reform, God-fearing and atheist, learned and ignorant, good and bad, saints and sinners, all were swept into the same death camps and the same crematoria. It has left – surely it must have left - a terrible, inerasable traumatic scar on Jewish consciousness. Perhaps in the bourgeois comforts of modern Britain we are in danger of forgetting it. Perhaps because discrimination falls most heavily on the coloured immigrants, we are in danger of forgetting it. Let us then remind ourselves of it – not only because it is a sign of moral weakness if we try to sweep it under the carpet – but without a sense of history, without an understanding of and a feeling for our destiny, we shall be a doomed group of little people without vision and with a trivial future.

The only other event in recent years that pulls us back to the recognition of the collective nature of Jewish destiny is the State of Israel. It sets before us the task and the possibility of creating a new Jewish life in a Jewish environment that can bridge the gap between the old and the new, and can provide a home and hope for the scattered tribes of Israel. Whether we agree with this or that particular policy of the Israeli Government is of secondary importance – it must not divide us in our efforts to strengthen the country and its institutions, and help to raise the standard of the under-privileged members of the population. Our support must be not only financial but also a demonstration of our emotional commitment to its future survival. As we have seen in the last debates at United Nations, when it comes to the crunch, the only true friend of Israel is the Jewish people itself. I hope you will all support the UIA as generously as you possibly can.

But our sense of history and the collective destiny of Jewry applies to other areas of Jewish involvement. I refer to the moral and practical support that we can give Jews in the Soviet Union, in Argentina and in other countries where Jews are discriminated against. And the collective destiny of the Jewish people wherever they may be affects us too – even in Cambridge – but of this I shall say no more.

But having stressed so strongly the collective destiny of Jews whatever their colour, political, social or religious complexion, I feel I must say something about the emergence in Cambridge of a specific Traditional Jewish Group. Jews who support traditional Judaism do not do so because they are better people. It would be an attitude of unforgivable arrogance for traditional Jews to claim that they are better than other people, especially when it would be most reprehensible even to contemplate such a thought on Yom Kippur. In this connection I cannot help quoting the words of the Baal Shem Tov - the founder of Chassidism – on the human tendency to feel superior to others. "When we detect an unfavourable quality in another person we do so because we possess it ourselves. Heaven arranges it in this way so that we should become aware of our own failings and be encouraged to seek repentance." A wonderful moral for Yom Kippur.

We are *not* better people but we have a different perception of Judaism. We see that what is important is continuity – change there may be but the emphasis remains on continuity – that is what tradition is about. And if we go back to examine those deviant movements that have emphasized change, we find that by and large they are people that have lost the sense of history. It is indeed one of the remarkable changes since the end of World War II that as these movements have recovered their sense of history, so they have moved closer to the pattern of traditional Judaism. Quite apart from the underlying religious concepts that may be involved, I think it is true to say that the broad sweep of history is on the side of traditional Judaism, of Rabbinic Judaism, and it is in that spirit that our congregation takes its stand.

We have in our congregation a number of very gifted and devoted members who will lead us, tonight and tomorrow, in a traditional Yom Kippur service with its traditional prayers, traditional tunes, traditional rituals and with an opportunity for all to participate. We shall be part of traditional Judaism throughout the world, taking part in such a service. I hope we shall all find here in the next twenty-four hours the environment that brings to life the spiritual message of self-examination that lies at the heart of the Yom Kippur service.

And now may I conclude on a lighter note that is also a more serious note? Last week I was reading a serious book on Chassidism and came across the following wonderful story told by a disciple. A great Chassidic rabbi was called at very short notice to a most important assembly on which the future peace of the Jewish communities in that region depended. To do this he had to make a very long journey - and time was too short. So by a miracle he made the horses travel like greased lightning.

The horses began to wonder. Usually they stopped en route and were given hay and water at various roadside inns. But this did not happen. The horses began to wonder. Surely, they thought, we are no longer horses but humans who only take their meals when they arrive at specific towns. But having passed through many towns without pausing anywhere to eat and drink, it occurred to them that they were no longer humans either, but they must be angels, for angels travel like lightning and do not eat.

When they arrived at their destination the horses were led into the stable, and when they saw the straw before them, they threw themselves on the fodder, *not* as angels, *not* as humans - but as horses.

And the rebbe added, "Fasting alone never turned a person into an angel – the real test is what we do after the fast."

May we all enter into the spirit of this Yom Kippur and draw from it the spiritual strength to sustain us in good deeds in the year to come. **נכתב נחתם בספר החיים לטובה** May we all be inscribed for good in the Book of Life.

Eve of Yom Kippur
Friday, 19th September 1980

O nce again we come together to celebrate Yom Kippur and the Honorary Officers of the congregation have asked me to say a few words of welcome. I am honoured to do so. Those of us who remember the consecration of this synagogue forty-three years ago by Rabbi Hertz - and there are not many left in this category – have a special feeling of regard for this synagogue as the religious and communal centre of our Jewish life. And so we rejoice to see this full and crowded assembly of old friends and faces from Cambridge residents, new residents, visitors from surrounding villages, visitors from farther afield, a few students and a few academics. Welcome to you all. We hope you will all share in the informality, the sincerity and the sense of involvement and participation that has always characterized our services here.

It is customary on this evening to make an appeal for financial support for Israel. It seems to me that this is right and proper, not only because this is one of those rare occasions where so many Jews are gathered together, but because it is appropriate that on a day which lies at the heart of our religious commitment we should demonstrate our support for the country which lies at the heart of our history and destiny as a people. The House of Israel must remain committed to the Home of Israel.

And this year I think we see more clearly than ever the growing antagonism in the Western world towards Israel, an antagonism which shows itself not only in a criticism of Israel's policies under Begin but in a more subtle form of weakening the rights of Israel to fair and secure borders. The political sell-out may become even more acute after the American Presidential elections. All these trends strengthen our recognition that when it comes to the crunch, the only true allies left to Israel are the Jewish people themselves. Our support must be not only financial, but also serve as a demonstration to Israel of our emotional commitment to its future survival. I hope you will all support the UIA as generously as you possibly can – all funds should be sent either to Dr Reif or to the Residents' Association.

But Yom Kippur was not instituted - as some people think – solely as a means of raising funds for Israel. Yom Kippur is a day of profound significance in the religious life of the Jew as an individual and as a Jew participating in corporate worship. We have in our congregation a number of very gifted and dedicated members who will lead us tonight and tomorrow with great devotion in a traditional Yom Kippur service, with its traditional prayers, tunes, rituals and ceremonials as part of a world-wide community taking part in such a service. We can all have the opportunity to participate and to feel part of traditional Israel at worship.

A few weeks ago my wife and I were in Southern California at a beautiful coastal resort known as La Jolla. We discovered a traditional synagogue not far from our hotel and there we celebrated Rosh Hashana. It was a traditional service which seemed endless, for it began at 9.00am and did not finish until 2.00pm, so that although we enjoyed it we also pined for the shorter, zippier service that we are used to in Cambridge. After a late lunch and a rest we went for a walk on the promenade and suddenly found ourselves surrounded by men and women and babies and children of all sizes and shapes converging on a table where stood a bearded rabbi handing out *kippot* [Hebrew: skullcaps] and stencilled copies of the Hebrew prayers. Before we knew what had happened, there were five hundred Jews of all types *davening mincha* [reciting the afternoon service], joining in the traditional *Kaddish* [Aramaic: 'holy'; mourner's prayer] and *Alenu* [Hebrew: 'It is incumbent upon us'; last prayer of the daily liturgy in most congregations] Rosh Hashana tunes. And then to the melody of an Israeli song we all marched to the water's edge where the Rabbi blew the *shofar* and recited *Tashlich*

[Hebrew; 'casting off'; prayers which involve symbolically casting off the previous year's sins into flowing water], while surrounding gentiles swam in the sea, balanced on surfboards and did their own thing. I might add that those who had done this before came with pockets full of cookies [and] old *matzohs* to cast on the water... And then we came back to dry land and recited the traditional *maariv* [evening] service for the eve of the second day Rosh Hashana. The whole episode was what the rabbi described as a unique religious happening in the south of California, but to me and my wife it made us realize the zest and joy with which an old ritual can be resuscitated and revivified so as to become a joyful experience.

We shall be exposed for the next twenty-four hours to a host of rituals and ceremonials, in all of which we can participate and it leads me to ask a simple fundamental question – what is the role of ritual in Jewish religious practice? Surely ritual is to provide the bridge between the abstract spiritual ideas of religion and the everyday world in which we live. As Solomon Schechter once said – Man does not live by O_2 alone. The rarefied atmosphere of intellectual and spiritual thought is not one in which we can survive for very long. We need concrete actions to identify with spiritual truths – this is the basis of our rituals and all our ceremonials and *mitzvot* [commandments]. They do not stand for themselves but for the ideas and ideals which lie behind them. They are a bridge but because of our limited understanding they can also become a barrier. Because it is often easier to carry out a ritual than to penetrate and contemplate what lies behind it, we are often in danger of seeing the ritual as something important in its own right. In that case it stands in the way of our understanding the truth which lies behind it. There is always this tension in our rituals and our traditions – on the one hand the bridge to spiritual ideas – on the other the barrier which we erect by glorifying the ritual into something greater than it really is. As Rabbi Mendel of Kotz, that great contentious thinker of Chassidic

Judaism, once said, "We must not make idols - we must not even make the *mitzvot* into idols."

God works behind the ritual

Rarely we raise the hem at this and that point and glimpse the Presence

We cannot grasp, we cannot hold the Vision which is the Presence

But we multiply the ritual.

Bridge and barrier are the twin characters of our rituals and our traditions. In the service in which we shall participate today and tomorrow, we shall be exposed to and inundated with traditional tunes, phrases, counterpoints, responses, prayers, sitting down and standing up, kneeling and bowing and listening to the *shofar*.

It is my prayer that in taking part in this unique service we shall, at some point, at this and that point, raise the hem and glimpse the spiritual message of our repentance and God's forgiveness that lies behind and the vision of a new year of good deeds for us and for all Israel. May we all be inscribed for good in the Book of Life: נכתב נחתם בספר החיים לטובה

Eve of Yom Kippur
Wednesday, 7*th* October 1981

Once again we come together to celebrate Yom Kippur and the Honorary Officers of the congregation have asked me to say a few words of welcome. I am glad to do so and honoured to be asked. As one who attended the consecration of this building forty-four years ago, I have a special feeling of regard for this synagogue as the religious and communal centre of our Jewish life. And so we rejoice to see this full and crowded assembly of old friends and faces of Cambridge residents, new residents, a few academics and particularly the students, many of whom are here for the first Cambridge experience of the Yom Kippur service. Welcome to you all. I hope you will all share in the informality, the sincerity and the sense of participation that have always characterized our services here.

I have been asked to say a few words about the tensions that now exist for all minorities in Britain. During the last couple of years there has been a great increase in violence on the streets and an upsurge of racial prejudice. Most of this is directed against the coloured communities that have settled in this country during the last twenty years or so. But some of it has overflowed and spilled against the Jews. Those who go round inciting hatred against blacks are the same people who can easily turn their bigotry against Jews. If any of you have any evidence of anti-Semitic activities in Cambridge or the dissemination of anti-Semitic literature, would you please provide this information to Maurice Bogen. He will pass it on to the Board of Deputies.

And because groups of Jews, conspicuously visible in public, can attract the attention of those who would like to make trouble I would ask you, if you do have to leave the synagogue building during the service, not to congregate in the forecourt.

You may know that there is a *midrash* [Hebrew: a homiletic story to explain a passage in the scriptures] which says that when the Temple was destroyed, the Holy One, blessed be He, scattered its stones all over the world and in every place where a stone fell, a House of Prayer was built. Thus every House of Prayer shares, in a modest way, the sanctity of the Temple. For this reason, added a nineteenth-century rabbinic authority, it shows a lack of respect, a lack of piety, if those who feel crowded in the synagogue forsake it to go out of doors. Thus rabbinic sensibility combines with communal prudence and suggests that we do not run out of the building and hang around in the front.

It is customary on this evening to make an appeal for financial support for Israel. It seems to me that this is right and proper – not only because this is one of those rare occasions when so many Jews come together – but because it is appropriate that on a day which lies at the heart of our religious commitment we should demonstrate our support for the country which lies at the heart of our history and destiny as a people. The House of Israel must remain committed to the Home of Israel.

I do not think any of us can foretell what the long-term consequences of yesterday's events in Egypt will be. But of one thing we can be sure – it will lead in the short-term to increased instability in the area, it will lead to a tremendous orchestration of all those forces in the Arab world that have opposed peace between Egypt and Israel, and this in turn will still further increase the pressure on Israel from pro-Arab countries. They only talk of what Israel has not done for the Arabs. They never mention the enormous risk Israel has taken in returning the Sinai peninsula to Egypt – for these pro-Arab countries, the right of Israel to fair and secure borders takes second place.

Of course all is not gloom. Even in Cambridge we sometimes hear more favourable words. Only a couple of months ago in Cambridge an ophthalmic specialist – a non-Jew - wrote to the local paper in these words, "I have only recently returned after working for six years in Israel among the Arab population. I have been struck by the hostile press that Israel is receiving both on television and other media..." and he goes on to add, "I am writing to ask for appreciation and understanding for a very courageous small nation to whose forbears we owe the very basis of our civilization, our code of justice, our love of truth and our concern for the individual." *Cambridge Evening News*, Monday 03.09.1981. My wife and I wrote to thank him for his letter and last week we received a reply. He has sold up his house in Cambridge and gone on *aliyah* [Hebrew: 'ascent'; the act of immigration to Israel] and he writes, "I think you will be glad to know that there is an increasing body of evangelical Christians like myself ... aware of our debt to Israel. This month about 3,000 will be coming here to celebrate simultaneously with all Jews the Festival of Tabernacles in Jerusalem, and also to make various public acts of identification. May the number grow greatly." So all is not gloom and doom. But in terms of world politics, I think we all now recognize that when it comes to the crunch the only reliable allies left to Israel are the Jewish people themselves. One most direct support must be financial, but by supplying this support we shall be demonstrating to Israel our emotional commitment to its future survival. As you know, the UIA is directing its main effort to a re-housing campaign in Ashkelon, and I hope you will all support the appeal as generously as you can. All contributions should be sent to Dr Reif or to the Jewish Residents' Association.

But however deeply we may feel the sickening uncertainty of events involving Israel and her neighbours, it would be wrong to concentrate all our thoughts on Middle Eastern politics. Yom Kippur is not a political demonstration. It is a religious demonstration of profound significance in the religious life of the Jew, both as an individual and as a Jew participating in corporate worship. We have in our congregation a number of very talented and dedicated members who will lead us tonight and tomorrow with great devotion in a traditional Yom Kippur service, with its traditional prayers, tunes, rituals and ceremonies. We can all take part in this service and feel that we are part of traditional Israel - or as Solomon Schechter would have said – Catholic Israel at worship.

Yom Kippur is a serious religious festival but it is not a sad one. Of course, it has its solemn and sombre episodes, but it is also a joyful and cheerful occasion, and this is part of a very old tradition which goes right back to Biblical times. How can one be joyous on such an occasion, you may ask? The Baal Shem Tov remarks that a man who loves his master will carry out even the most disagreeable tasks with good cheer and even joyfully. So we may make our confessions and offer our prayers with good cheer and good spirits.

But because our hearts may be too full of sombre thoughts may I lighten your spirits with a short anecdote from Agnon's book *Days of Awe*. It is the story of a simple Jew who on the Eve of Yom Kippur settles his account with God. Here - he says to the Lord of the Universe - is the list I kept scrupulously of all my offences against You in the course of the year and here, Lord of the Universe, is the list I've been keeping of all the afflictions, all the *tsorres* [Yiddish: troubles], all the loses You've put us through this year. If a proper bookkeeping be made, I'm afraid I've been more sinned against than sinning. But this is Yom Kippur eve when we are all obliged to forgive one another. So, Lord of the Universe, I forgive You and You will forgive us for all the sins we have sinned against You. And then, because he is a simple man, he does not know how to conclude his account with God. It is always difficult to end a discourse. There are Rabbis who give sermons every week who know how to begin but never know how to end. How much more difficult then for a simple Jew who is addressing the Almighty. All he can think of is the only greeting he can express – and so according to Agnon he ends this debate with the phrase *Le-chayim* – to life! What an inspired greeting – to life.

May we all be inscribed in the Book of Life:

בספר חיים נזכר ונכתב לפניך אנחנו וכל עמך בית ישראל
לחיים טובים ושלום.

[Hebrew: May we all be inscribed and sealed in the Book of Life in Your Presence, we and all Your people of the House of Israel, with the blessing of a good life and peace] – Amen.

Erev Yom Kippur
Sunday 26th September 1982

It is customary on this evening to make an appeal for financial support for Israel. It has always seemed to me, if done in proper measure, that this is right and proper – not only because this is one of those rare occasions when so many Jews are gathered together – because it is appropriate that on a day which lies at the heart of our religious commitment we should demonstrate our support for the country which lies at the heart of our history and destiny as a people. The House of Israel must remain committed to the Home of Israel.

Yet I do not know of any occasion since the establishment of Israel when Jews both inside the country and outside have been so divided, so confused and so bewildered. The invasion of Lebanon to clear out the PLO received wide support, though not everybody approved of it. It involved the shelling of quarters in which many of the PLO had mounted their guns, rockets and tanks and in the process many innocent civilians were killed. Does the moral responsibility for these civilian deaths fall on Israel or does it fall on the PLO who exploited the situation? On these issues let me remind you that in the liberation of the Falkland Islands, Falkland islanders during one crucial attack were killed by British shells. Innocent casualties in military bombardment are a terrible but apparently unavoidable feature of modern war. Whether Israel should have *persisted* in the way she did produced a wide split in Jewish opinion – but in a democratically elected system decisions are made and acted upon. Those of us who remember the pre-war years in Britain will recall the tremendous split in public opinion over Munich, although Chamberlain's decisions were the expressions of a democratically elected majority. I would have spoken of this if Yom Kippur had occurred twelve days ago and I would have discussed the moral and political dilemmas involved. We shall see more of them when the Reagan plan is discussed and the future of the Palestinians in Samaria and the Gaza Strip again comes up for reconsideration.

But an event took place in Beirut that has shaken us all. Israeli troops on guard around a refugee camp in Beirut, stationed there to prevent bloodshed and disorder, allowed a group of barbaric militiamen who are supposed to be Christians to enter the camp. There was a massacre of women and children. The reporting of this event and indeed most of all the other aspects of the Israeli activities in Lebanon by the media has been so vicious and malevolent that one would think that the murderers had been Israelis. They were Christians and we still have to hear a word from the Archbishop of Canterbury, the Maronite Archbishop and from the Pope condemning in specific terms the murderous barbarism of their adherents. The hostile reporting has, of course, influenced us all. On the one hand we have become more defensive. Some of us have had the moral courage to express some criticism of Israel but on the whole have avoided public statements that will add comfort and support to our enemies. The fact is that the murders were not carried out by Israelis, that in the Lebanese civil war 100,000 Christians and Moslems were slaughtered and hardly a word was said by those inspired newspaper reporters who now find every opportunity to vilify us. And yet, my friends, there remains amongst us all a sense of shame that Israel should somehow through naivety, stupidity, through having the wrong Lebanese friends, have got involved in this business. Those young men who could have been at home with their families or at synagogue celebrating the Jewish New Year were acting as guardians of peace while a massacre took place.

We would not be worthy of our Jewish heritage if we did not feel a terrible sense of shame.

No doubt some Jews will enjoy self-flagellation. But we would do better to recall the tremendous achievements of Israel: the extent to which it has reclaimed the desert, provided homes for Jews from the war camps of Europe, from the ghettos of Arabia, from the prisons of Soviet Russia, and even Jews from more comfortable Western lands. We recall the agriculture, the industry, the science, the technology that have flourished, the institutes of higher learning, the enormous flowering of Jewish studies, the hitherto unblemished record of the Israel Defence Force. We can look back on these achievements with pride, and in the face of so much current hostility we can say to Israel: we are behind you. For this reason I in no way qualify my original request that you support the current United Israel Appeal. Israel needs our help – I think it also needs our prayers.

But my friends, however deeply we may feel sickened by the latest events in Israel it would be wrong to concentrate all our thoughts on the Middle East. Yom Kippur is not a political demonstration. It is a religious demonstration of profound significance in the life of the Jew, both as an individual and as a Jew participating in corporate worship. If we cannot get Israel out of our minds today to find at least a few corners for other thoughts, we shall have committed a betrayal of our religious heritage – we shall have allowed the State of Israel to block our access to the message of Yom Kippur. As the great maverick Chassidic Rabbi Menachem Mendel of Kotz said to his congregants: the greatest sin is to create idols – you must not make idols, not even of *mitzvot*, not even of Israel.

We must find room in our hearts and thoughts for the real purpose of this Day of Assembly – a solemn stocktaking of our sins of omission and commission. Not long ago I read a short history of the Greeks, that most marvellous of people of the ancient world whose philosophy and art and science find no parallel among their contemporaries. But when I read of their religious ideas I was amazed at their primitive, almost barbaric, nature. The world was ruled by an Olympian family, Zeus, Hera, Athena, Artemis, Apollo and the rest: and side by side with lustful characters there was a cult of Nature Goddesses with mystical rituals, orgiastic rites, ecstatic dances, emblematical processions. At the time when Homer and his contemporaries were writing their great historic odes, Moses had already been dead for five hundred years, King David for two hundred years – these epic writers were in fact almost contemporary with Amos and Isaiah. Think of that vast contrast between these immensely gifted pagans and the simple majestic monotheism of the Jews. Think of the pantheon of the immoral gods and goddesses, think of the way they deified their kings as subjects of worship and compare that with the Jewish view that a king has rights only if he is faithful to God's laws. Compare the Greeks' scorn of foreigners – the barbarian – with Amos's inspired vision of all people, even your enemies, being equal in God's eyes. Compare the glorification of the mythological and barbaric wars in Homer's *Iliad* with Isaiah who in the same century is already preaching of a new moral order in which nation would speak unto nation. This is the same Isaiah who in tomorrow's *Haftorah* talks of repentance and renewal, who scorns our fasting and hypocritical self-affliction, who demands righteousness in place of wickedness and oppression.

Three centuries later Greek philosophy blossomed and took into its compass the concepts of ethics, morals, virtue, the good: yet it always remained an intellectual exercise which provided no pattern for day-to-day conduct. And in spite of its tremendous achievements, the Greek approach to morals breaks through another dimension that distinguishes it from Judaism. Basically, the Hellenistic beliefs are fatalistic and pessimistic – man is always at the whim of the gods – of the spirits, of the wind, of the sea, of the sun: if man speaks or if he doesn't speak, if he does something, if he does nothing – he is powerless and doomed.

Judaism is basically a religion of optimism and hope. It believes in God and it believes in man. Through the genius of the rabbis it found its practical formulation in the codes and practices that we call *mitzvot* – disciplines that can help us lead the moral life. It developed into a remarkable synthesis of religious belief, prophetic vision and ritual practices that in turn produced what one might call Jewish religious humanism; and it is this that has imparted a sense of an ethical and moral order that has set its stamp on the Jewish people for all time. There is no room for barbarism in Judaism.

Last week I spoke to a woman friend who survived the death camps at Auschwitz. I do not need to talk of the suffering, of the butchery, of the massacre of innocent men, women and children. You have seen something of this on TV or you have read about it, or have met people who have experienced it. My friend told me that in their blackest moods, when bestiality seemed to have reached its absolute limit, she and her group took an oath that if they survived the death camp the first thing they would do, each and every one of them, would be to murder an innocent German child. They somehow survived the death camp; not one of them murdered a German child. Thank God Jews are not barbarous – I pray it should always be so.

Yom Kippur is an occasion in which we try, through our centuries-old ceremonies, rituals, songs and melodies to consider our failings. Practically all the sins are moral ones. Let us concentrate on them within the framework of the service and respond to the moral challenge, to recall our past failings and to assert that, with God's help, we will do better.

Let me conclude with a passage from the liturgy: Lord of the Universe – fulfil the wishes of our hearts, yield our desires and grant our petition – pardon all our sins, our iniquities with loving kindness and mercy. Purify us from our sins, our iniquities, our shame and our transgression and remember us with a good remembrance. Grant us salvation and compassion and remember us for a long and honourable life for peace and sustenance and support.

Eve of Yom Kippur
Friday, 16th October 1983

Once again we come together in this synagogue, the religious and communal centre of Cambridge, to celebrate Yom Kippur and I have been asked to say a few words of welcome. I am glad and honoured to do so. As one who has attended the consecration of this building forty-five years ago, I have a special feeling of regard and affection for this synagogue as the religious and communal centre of our Jewish life here. And so we all rejoice to see this fairly crowded assembly of old friends and faces of Cambridge residents, new residents, visitors from surrounding villages, visitors from further afield, no students alas, but even a few academics. Welcome to you all. We have in this congregation...dedicated members who will lead us tonight and tomorrow in a traditional Yom Kippur service and I hope that you will all share in the informality, the sincerity and sense of involvement by the congregation that has always characterized our services here. Every individual who becomes an active participant in the services helps his neighbour to participate and makes the service a whole experience shared by everybody.

It is customary on this evening to make an appeal for financial support for Israel. It seems always to me, if done in proper measure, that it is right and proper, not only because this is one of those rare occasions when so many Jews are gathered together, but because it is appropriate that on a day which lies at the heart of our religious commitment, we should demonstrate our support for the country that lies at the heart of our history and destiny as a people. The House of Israel must remain committed to the Home of Israel.

This Yom Kippur marks the 10th anniversary of the Yom Kippur War, the attack on Israel by Egypt, Syria and Jordan, that almost succeeded in cutting the country in two. And although in the end, with much loss of life and limb, Israel emerged intact, the Yom Kippur War has left its mark on Israeli attitudes to defence, security, Arab neighbours and the West Bank to this very day. One of its consequences, though it may not have been inevitable, was the military campaign known as Peace in Galilee. The campaign is still going on.

This time last year we were all divided, confused and bewildered by events in Lebanon and embarrassed to the point of shame by the Christian massacres in Shatila – an event that Israel had the moral guts to investigate and to apportion responsibility – an event which not one leading Christian dignitary had the moral courage to condemn. As to the present situation, I fear that it will be a long time before Israel can safely disengage itself from Lebanon, and say Peace in Galilee has been achieved.

But I do not want to talk tonight about military campaigns, Samaria and Judea, party politics, Sephardim and Askenazim, Peace now or Peace later, nor even about the depressing economic situation in Israel.

I would like us instead to remind ourselves that Israel is a home for Jews who want to leave their present country: whether to escape physical persecution, economic harassment, social discrimination or even just to be able to live their lives as Jews. Indeed, in the last thirty-six years, thousands upon thousands of Jews have fled from Arab countries where they were doomed, thousands have left the enforced assimilation of Soviet Russia, thousands have left the virulent anti-Semitism of South America, and in the last decade many Jews from Western Europe have grown tired of living in the interstices of a tolerant but alien culture and have gone on *aliyah*. It is not always enough to be a Jew at home and a man of the world abroad. In Israel the Jew is a Jew both at home and abroad. The boundaries of his identity are greatly extended. He really and truly is at home...

A few months ago my wife and I were on holiday in Majorca and got into conversation with a young Spaniard. He noticed my wife's *Magen David* and mentioned that he had just spent six months in Israel on a kibbutz and had even learned a little Hebrew. A few further comments led us to ask if he was Jewish. "Not exactly," he replied. Apparently, three hundred years ago the whole Majorcan Jewish population had been faced with the choice of conversion or death. They chose conversion. "It is true," he said, "that we have been Catholics for centuries but everybody knows that our village is really Jewish. Next year I hope to go to Israel again – probably I will stay there for good."

It seems...that three hundred years of Catholicism had not enabled him to find his true identity. I don't know if our *rabbonim* will help, but Israel provides him with a route by which he can recover his identity and be at ease with his Jewishness. Israel will be home for him.

I hope you will all contribute as generously as you can to this year's UIA.

But of course it is not only of Israel as a country that I wish to speak this evening. Today is the most important day in the religious calendar of Israel as a people. Yom Kippur speaks to us and appeals both to our heart and to our head. To our heart because all its ceremonies, its tunes, its ritual, even our getting up and sitting down are filled with associations of past years, of contacts with our parents and grandparents, our feeling of being part of a holy day that is being celebrated by Jews all over the world and has been so celebrated for well over two thousand years. But it also appeals to our minds for our prayers are not merely familiar tunes. They contain words, and these words are a constant challenge.

I would like to discuss one of these.

Rabbinic Judaism regards man and woman as creatures of flesh and blood, with senses and passions but also with what we might call a spark of the divine that distinguishes us from the animal world. Yom Kippur makes us think more deeply of this part of our nature. One way is by considering our sins. It has always been part of this tradition to ask our neighbours for forgiveness for any offence or injury that we may have caused them, for injustice can only be forgiven by the person who has been subjected to it. If you have wronged your neighbour, nobody, not even God, can forgive you – only the neighbour himself.

Nevertheless, when we look at the list of sins in the *Al Chet* [Hebrew: 'For the sin'] prayers, sins that we ask God to forgive us, we find, that apart from moral sins, many of them are offences against our neighbours. Sins of violence, of evil speech, of usury, of arrogance, of envy, of cheating, of tale bearing, of hatred. These are not theological sins. They are not ritual sins and at first sight they seem to have little to do with God. Yet we confess them as sins against God

על חטא שחטנו לפניך [Hebrew: for the sins which we have sinned against You] and ask His forgiveness. I think the answer is simple though unexpected. Every time we say bitchy things about a man we do not like, we do not harm him, but we diminish ourselves: every time we look with envy on our neighbour we do not harm him but we degrade ourselves. In lowering ourselves we diminish the divine spark within us, we expel a little of God's presence. That is why we must ask His forgiveness and pray that he will restore it to us so that with His help the mouth that spoke evil of his neighbour may speak well of him, the eye that regarded him with envy may rejoice in his success, the brow that looked with arrogance may look with forbearing, the heart that thumped with passion and anger may beat with compassion and love, the ear that revels in hearing evil talk may turn to other themes: it is, after all, the same ear that heard God's voice on Mount Sinai.

In reciting the *Al Chet* we confess to God that we have sinned in diminishing ourselves: we pray that the process may be reversed and that part of the *Shechinah* [Hebrew: Divine Presence] may be restored to us. This is a challenge but we should not be afraid, because for reasons known only to God, Judaism is a religion of optimism and hope.

I wish you all כתיבה וחתימה טובה [Hebrew: May we all be inscribed and sealed in the Book of Life].

Erev Yom Kippur
Friday 5th October 1984

O nce more we have come together in this synagogue to celebrate Yom Kippur. It is a great honour for me to welcome you all here. We all rejoice to see this crowded assembly of old friends and faces from Cambridge residents, though alas some are no longer with us, new residents, visitors from surrounding villages, visitors from further afield – Israel and America – and, of course, students. Welcome to you all. We hope you will all share in the informality, the sincerity and the sense of involvement and participation by the worshippers themselves that have always characterized our services here.

It is customary on this evening to make an appeal for financial support for Israel. It has always seemed to me that, if done in proper measure, it is right and proper that we should do so.

Israel is going through a very difficult phase in all aspects of its life and I will not turn this into a political occasion. I would instead refer to one aspect that affects all of us who live outside Israel: that is the hostile reporting that still continues in much of the serious press. There are some papers and correspondents who seem to take a malicious delight in criticizing the country and drag in barbed references whenever they can. My friends tell me that this is part of a pro-Arab movement to de-legitimize the State of Israel. I see it in simpler terms as a certain hatred of the State. And if I translate this into Hebrew it acquires another dimension. For hatred of Israel in Hebrew is *Sinat Yisrael*, and *Sinas Yisroel* for countless generations has been the classical Hebrew phrase for anti-Semitism.

I do recognize that one can be totally critical of Israel without being anti-Semitic but the distinction is a fine one and I think we are all aware of it. However, I do not wish to pursue this issue: instead I wanted to say that the Jewish antidote to *Sinat Yisrael*, hate of Israel, is *Ahavat Yisrael* - love of Israel. *Ahavas Yisroel* has been a Jewish virtue extolled by the rabbis throughout the ages. It has ramifications that touch on every aspect of Jewish life, social, political, communal, religious, ethical. This evening I can only refer to its bearing on the State of Israel – it means the following: we may consider the war in Lebanon a disastrous mistake, the settlements in Judea and Samaria as illiberal and unjust, the ravings of a Rabbi who speaks the language of Enoch Powell as indefensible, the management of the economy as *meshuggah* [Hebrew/Yiddish: crazy], and the loss of morale in the country as a whole as deplorable. *Ahavat Yisrael* means that whatever our views on these issues may be, the world should know and Israel should know that the House of Israel stands firmly behind the Homeland of Israel. We are Israel's true and constant friend in good times and bad.

I hope you will all support the United Israel Appeal as generously as you can.

And now I would like to leave this and turn to the real purpose of Yom Kippur – the Day of Atonement. The last dozen years or more I have spoken on this theme and it may be that the time has come for other members of the community to say their piece. I hope, therefore, that you will bear with me for a few minutes if I tell you how it all came about. In the past the community was poor in synagogal talent …[omitted section]… and we advertised and bought in a paid cantor to conduct the Services for the High Festivals. Twelve years ago we had a *Baal T'filah* [Hebrew: lit. "master of prayer"] who performed very well and after Kol Nidre asked if he could give a short talk. We agreed. To our astonishment it consisted solely of a rather vulgar huckstering appeal for financial support for Israel as though that were the sole purpose of Yom Kippur. Mr. Ratner, who was Synagogue secretary at the time, was very distressed and asked me to add a few words about Yom Kippur itself. On subsequent years I was asked to continue both themes – support for Israel and something about Yom Kippur – and that is how you have been stuck with me on Kol Nidre night for the last twelve years.

Of course, the situation now is very different, and we have in the congregation gifted and dedicated members who conduct our services with great expertise throughout the year: they will lead us tonight and tomorrow in our traditional Yom Kippur Service.

If I looked back at the themes which I spoke about I find that sometimes they were evoked by some particular event in Jewish or world affairs, or some lecture I had attended. Last year, finding myself surrounded by widespread malicious tittle-tattle and gossip about a community member, I tried to talk moralistically about the sin of evil talk – *Loshen Hora* – לשון הרע. Needless to say it was a mistaken effort and the tittle-tattle continued as before. More often I find that my talks have been based on some single phrase or poem, or some unusual essay. For example, a few months ago I came across a short poem which read:

Although it may be true that as the Greek philosopher said

That man is the true measure of all things
Man, like patriotism, however noble,
Is not enough.

Here, in less than thirty words lies, I think, the basis of the religious impulse.

More relevant is the following comment which I came across: it directly concerns Yom Kippur. It refers to the very last words of the service. Tomorrow evening when we come to the final words of the final closing prayer – the *Neilah* – we repeat seven times ה הוא האלהים [Hebrew: "The Lord, He is God"]. And the comment is as follows: the first word for 'the Lord' which it would be improper for me to repeat in Hebrew is, according to rabbinic tradition, the word that is used throughout the Bible and our liturgy to refer to God in His attributes of mercy and loving kindness; the second word is the one according to rabbinic tradition which refers to God in His attribute of justice. Consequently we are saying more than "The Lord is God". We are affirming that the God of mercy and loving kindness is the God of justice. It seems to me that after a day in which we have confessed our sins, this is a remarkable confession of our faith. I might add that this comment which is, of course, implicit in the ancient rabbinic traditions was made by a man who spent the war years in a Nazi concentration camp.

But more generally I find that, although by temperament and background I am a long way from Chassidim, I have used quotations from Chassidic sources. The reason is clear. The Chassidic masters rediscovered the parable and there is no better way of fixing a moral truth in our minds. My favourite parable is one I related four or five years ago and as you will not hear it again from me from this place I am going to repeat it. It deals with the following problem: to what extent does one day of fasting and prayer affect our conduct for the rest of the year? The rebbe tells the following:

Two hundred years ago there was a wonder rabbi in Eastern Europe. One morning he heard that the king of the neighbouring state was about to issue, that very afternoon, an edict expelling all the Jews from his country and confiscating their property. Only the wonder rabbi could prevent this. So he asked his coachman to harness the horses. "It is a three day journey," said the coachman, "we will never make it in time." "Never mind," said the master and off they went, streaking through the countryside like greased lightning. The horses began to talk to one another. "Usually," they said, "we stop at various wayside inns for food and water, but we are not stopping." Perhaps, they thought, we are not horses but men who only stop at larger hostelries. But they swept past hostelry after hostelry without stopping. Perhaps, thought the horses, we are not men but princes – for princes stop at only the most prestigious castles. But on they swept faster and faster without stopping at any castles. Finally the truth dawned on the horses. "Surely," they said, "we have become as angels; for only angels can travel so far and so fast without food and drink and without rest." And so they swept on and arrived at the king's palace just in time. The wonder rabbi dismounted, had an audience with the king and persuaded him to withdraw his edict. The Jews were saved.

As to the horses, they were unharnessed and led into the stables. As soon as they saw the fodder in front of them they fell upon it, not as angels, not as princes, not as men, but as horses.

And the rebbe remarks, a long fast may make you feel angelic but the real test of your real self is how you behave when you return to ordinary life and the work-a-day world around you.

I wish you all a כתיבה וחתימה טובה [Hebrew: May we all be inscribed and sealed for good in the Book of Life].

Erev Yom Kippur
Tuesday 24 September 1985

O nce more we have come together to take part in the Yom Kippur service: and it is a great honour and privilege for me to welcome you here, local residents who come often – or rarely - visitors from neighbouring villages, no students alas! but visitors from overseas, especially Israel and America. Welcome to you all. During the last year I attended several synagogues in Europe and America but coming back to Cambridge I experience and enjoy once again the special flavour of our synagogue service, a quality that has indeed characterized it since I have known it over the past fifty years – the full and committed participation of the congregation. I hope you will all share as full partners in our service, expertly led by dedicated members of our community.

It is customary in this country to make an appeal on Kol Nidre night for support for Israel. I think it is right and proper that we should do so, for if Yom Kippur represents the central event in the religious experience of the Jew, Israel represents the central hope – yet to be fulfilled – of our future as a people. This year Israel's need is greater than ever. The economic situation, unemployment, security, international relations all raise enormous problems. The money that we contribute to Israel is not only a material help – it is a demonstration to ourselves and to the Israelis that we are committed to the future of the State.

I do not like raising political issues on Yom Kippur, but there is one theme I would like to raise briefly that, at first sight, appears political. I refer to the double standards adopted by the Press and TV in this country and in most of Western Europe in relation to Israel and her neighbours. Whenever some issue arises for which Israel can be criticized it is announced in screaming headlines and articulated in harsh and often malicious terms. By comparison criticisms of Arab affairs are muted and restrained. There is no doubt that double standards are adopted. Why should this be so? No doubt part of it reflects a genuine pro-Palestinian sentiment: part of it arises from a wish to maintain favourable relations with the richer Arab States – no longer because of oil but because the West is seeking markets for their industrial products, consumer goods and especially arms – and if it is not Britain today it will certainly be France tomorrow; and a third reason may simply be that reporters do not like Israel or the Jews. But if we strip away the pro-Palestinian sentiment, the pro-Arab bias, the possible anti-Semitism, there remains an important element that the reporters themselves may not be fully aware of. It seems to me that at the base of it all is their feeling that Israel and the Jews are a civilized people and that the highest standards are to be expected – sometime indeed they expect an impossibly high standard.

By contrast, what lies at the base of their attitudes to Arabs is the tacit view that one shouldn't expect anything better. And if this is so it seems to me that it would be a sad day for Israel and the Jews in general if double standards were to be dropped and we were to be judged by the same indifference, the same spiritual apathy, the same moral insensitivity with which the Arab massacres in Lebanon or in Iran or in Iraq or in Damascus are reported.

So if we feel irritated by the hostile and critical tone of the press and the radio we can draw comfort from the underlying assumptions that we have standards, that we should live by them and that we are expected to live by them. In this sense the issue is a moral, not a political, one. And it is our sense of commitment to these moral values that binds us together with what is best for Israel.

I hope you will support the appeal as generously as possible.

But Yom Kippur was not instituted simply as a fund-raising occasion. It is the most important event in the Jewish calendar. It is a day of spiritual stocktaking and it is expressed in age-old prayers, ceremonials, melodies, *shofar*-blowing, standing up, sitting down, prostrating oneself, opening and closing of the Ark. All of this is to induce in us a spirit of contrition, a reminder of how we failed our better selves, a hope that we may do better.

There are many theories of prayer but I am not a theologian and this is not the occasion to discuss them. But all of us at some time or other ask what our prayers achieve and whether they are ever answered. Rabbi Jonathan Sacks once gave a rather light-hearted comment on this. Some prayers, he said, are answered straight away. If we pray that we may win the football pool the answer is *immediate* - it is usually No! But our Yom Kippur prayers are not of this type. Most of them are in the form of hymns of praise, pleas for spiritual help, confessions of wrongdoing. And it seems to me that we can obtain a fresh insight into our Yom Kippur service by thinking of the meaning of the verb to pray. In Hebrew it is להתפלל: [*lehitpalel*]; it is the reflexive form of the root פלל [*palal*]. Now, Hebrew is an ancient language and words often have changing meanings. But one of the oldest meanings of פלל is to judge. Indeed, Yom Kippur, which is the Day of Judgment and is called *Yom HaDin* could, in classical Hebrew, have been called *Yom P'lilah*. So that, as a friend of mine recently pointed out to me, one possible translation of התפלל, that is 'to pray', is to judge oneself, to be engaged in self-judgment. It seems to me that this is a meaning most appropriate to the Yom Kippur service. For we are primarily engaged during the service precisely in this task. And if you ask if our prayers are answered, it is surely that in judging ourselves we are well on the way to repentance, and if we are on the way to repentance we are well on the way to obtaining forgiveness. And the *machzor* helps us on this path for it describes in detail, over and over again, how we have failed.

All this sounds very serious and indeed Yom Kippur is a most serious religious event – but it is not a sad one. For although it has its solemn and sombre episodes it is also a festival, as our Rabbis tell us it is a joyful and optimistic occasion, as many of our Yom Kippur melodies show – it is a day of hope and conciliation.

And so allow me to lighten your hearts with a short anecdote from Agnon's marvellous book *Days of Awe*. It is a story of a simple Jew who, on the eve of Yom Kippur, settles his account with God:

Here – he says to the Lord of the Universe - is the list I kept scrupulously of all my offences against You in the course of the year; and here, Lord of the Universe, is the list of all the afflictions, all the *tsorres* [Yiddish: troubles], all the losses You have put us through this year. If a proper bookkeeping be made, I'm afraid I've been more sinned against than sinning. But this is Yom Kippur eve, when we are all obliged to forgive one another. So, Lord of the Universe, I forgive You, and You will forgive us for all the sins we have sinned against You.

He is a simple man. He does not know how to end his account with God. All he can think of is the only greeting he knows – and so he ends his discourse, his prayer, his act of self-judgment with the final greeting – *Lechayim* – to life!

בספר חיים נזכר ונכתב לפניך אנחנו וכל עמך בית ישראל
לחיים טובים ולשלום.

May we all be inscribed in the Book of Life, we and all Thy people of the House of Israel, with the blessing of a good life and with peace and reconciliation, Amen.

I wish you all a כתיבה וחתימה טובה [Hebrew: May we all be inscribed and sealed for good in the Book of Life].

Erev Yom Kippur
Sunday 12th October 1986

Once again we come together in this synagogue to celebrate Yom Kippur. It is a great honour and privilege for me to welcome you all here - old friends and faces from Cambridge residents, new residents, visitors from surrounding villages, visitors from further afield especially Israel and America and, last but not least, the students for whom this synagogue was originally built. Welcome to you all. We hope you will experience the special flavour of our service and become part of it as full and active participants.

In Cambridge today there are over two hundred Jewish families, a large number of committed Jewish students and even a few university dons who are involved in synagogal and community affairs. But when this synagogue was dedicated by Chief Rabbi Hertz forty-nine years ago there were only six resident Jewish families in Cambridge, practically no Jewish dons in Jewish affairs and to those of us who were students at the time the building seemed positively palatial – small wonder that it is now bursting at the seams.

On the outside of the synagogue is a brass plaque that we inherit from earlier days and which bears the inscription "Cambridge Hebrew Congregation". It takes us back to times when Anglo-Jewry was self-conscious and glad to use a synonym that both described and disguised its Jewish identity. Today our attitudes to Jewish identity are very different – for three reasons. The first is the Holocaust; the second is the growing interest among young Jews in Jewish and Judaistic studies; the third is the emergence of the State of Israel.

The State of Israel certainly fills a very large part of Jewish consciousness today and it is customary on this evening to make an appeal for financial support for it. I think that it is right and proper that we should do so for, if Yom Kippur represents the central event in the religious experience of the Jew, Israel represents the central hope – still to be fulfilled – of our future as a people. Israel is always going through some difficult phase. Today it is not only faced by enemies on many fronts, by a world-press that is often partisan and hostile, it is also faced by internal tensions that are a source of great worry to the *Yishuv* [Hebrew: settlement; the Jewish community in Israel] and to Jewry outside.

No Jew can be happy – I *hope* no Jew can be happy - at the polarization that has developed to such an extent between the secular and orthodox communities. But this is no reason for withdrawing our support. We should do better to remind ourselves of the positive achievements of Israel in the thirty-eight years of its existence, achievements that compare not unfavourably with those of States ten times older and more established – but then we should remember that as a people we are almost one hundred times older than the State itself. Israel has built up the country, developed its agriculture, its industry, its educational institutions and above all it has provided a home and proud identity for the Jew wherever he comes from, whatever the colour of his skin. Our financial contributions mean more than material help – they demonstrate to Israel and to ourselves that we are committed to the future of our past, to the future of Israel and to the House of Israel.

I hope you will all support the appeal as generously as possible.

But Yom Kippur was not instituted simply as a means of raising funds. It is the most important day in the religious calendar of the Jew. It is a day of spiritual stocktaking and it appeals to both our heart and our head. To our heart because all its ceremonies, its tunes, its rituals, our getting up and sitting down, the opening and closing of the Ark, the blowing of the *shofar* are filled with associations of past years, of contacts with our parents and grandparents, with our children, our feeling of being part of a holy day that is being celebrated by Jews all over the world and has been celebrated for countless generations. But it [also] appeals to our minds and intellects for our prayers are not only tunes but contain words that are a constant challenge.

Last year I suggested that we might gain fresh insight into our Yom Kippur Service by thinking of the meaning of the verb to pray. In Hebrew it is להתפלל – it is the reflexive form of the word פלל, and one of the oldest meanings of this word is to judge. So we may think of להתפלל that is, to pray as to judge oneself – to be engaged in self-judgment. And that is a meaning most appropriate to the Yom Kippur Service.

I would like to pursue this thought with a very short Chassidic story. It concerns the first chapter of Genesis. After Eve and then Adam had eaten the forbidden fruit they were ashamed of their nakedness; Genesis III, 8: "And they heard the voice of the Lord God walking in the garden towards the cool of the day and the man and his wife hid themselves amongst the trees of the garden. And the Lord God called unto the man and said unto him: 'Where art thou? איכה.'"

The founder of the Chabad movement, Reb Shneur Zalman ben Baruch of Ladi, was asked: Why did God ask such a pointless question? Can you imagine that God the Omniscient, the All-knowing, did not know where Adam was? The Rebbe replied: God knew, Adam didn't know. This aspect of self-knowledge, of asking ourselves where we are, who we are, what we stand for is in one sense the central theme of the Yom Kippur Service – it is part of our quest for self-judgment.

Throughout our lives we cover our nakedness with all sorts of protective layers or shells – I hesitate to use the word *klippot* which has a different flavour – with possessions, with activities, with positions in the community and in society, with circles of friends, with family circles, with accomplishments in business or in the professions, with hobbies all to protect our inner selves. Some of us follow the advice of the rabbis and gird ourselves with *Torah* study and *mitzvot.* Evidently not all of these coverings are of equal value. But whatever the garment in which we are clothed, beneath the garment lies the naked Adam hiding from his God and his own conscience.

Abraham Herschel, rabbi, scholar and mystic, once said of the trappings with which we build up our own persona, and our feverish scurrying to and fro to keep our minds off things that really matter, that we are like messengers who have forgotten the message, who we really are, what [ ] the whole affair [is] about.

The answer lies in the question addressed to Adam. *Adam ayeka?* Adam, do you know where you are and who you are?

Yom Kippur is a serious day but it is also a festive day full of hope and optimism. In following the Service, expertly led by dedicated members of our community, may we find with the help of the *machzor* our way to self-knowledge. For this provides the path to repentance and if we are well on the way to repentance we may well be on the way to obtaining forgiveness.

Let me conclude with a composite prayer from the *machzor*:

Lord of the Universe – fulfil the wishes of our hearts for good, pardon our iniquities with loving kindness and mercy. Purify us from our sins, from our shame, from our transgressions and remember us with a good remembrance. And may we be inscribed in the Book of Life, we and all Thy people of the House of Israel with the blessing of a good life, with peace and reconciliation. Amen.

I wish you all גמר חתימה טובה [Hebrew: May our prayers come to a good conclusion].

Erev Yom Kippur
Friday 2nd October 1987

On this important occasion it is a great honour for me, once again, to say a few words. They fall into three parts: words of welcome, words about support for Israel, and thoughts about Yom Kippur itself.

The easiest part is to welcome you all. This year we celebrate the fiftieth year of the foundation of this synagogue. A jubilee event which was marked by a remarkable gathering in Cambridge three weeks ago of former Cambridge alumni. It was marvellous for some of us who are old-timers to meet people we had not seen for half a century – as well as later students. The event was crowned by a brilliant address by Abba Eban, who had been the founding President of the Cambridge University Jewish Society in 1937, the year in which this building was consecrated.

But the celebration marked more than a date in the calendar. The world fifty years ago was a very different place from the world today in general terms and especially as regards Jews. This is not the time or place to deal with the moral and political decline of Britain and France in those days and the anguish students and others felt at the supine indifference to what Hitler and Mussolini were doing. Many of my Jewish contemporaries were swept away by the illusion of a just and noble communist society.

Those of us who were committed Zionists were spurred to greater activity by our direct contact with the new wave of refugees who were arriving from Europe. As the years moved towards 1939 the sense of crisis increased, though none of us could have foreseen the terrible tragedy that was to consume the whole of European Jewry.

In that period our main aim was to save Jews and the Jewish people. Fifty years later with the Jewish homeland –

the State of Israel – securely established I sense a different aim amongst the committed Jewish students we meet in this synagogue. They are more concerned with saving Judaism and maybe themselves.

If I look back to 1937 I see that in spite of the turbulent times which we were experiencing and in spite of our wide differences, the Student Society and the new synagogue provided a haven of religious, cultural, social and political togetherness. I think that we realized that we were all ultimately in the same boat. A tradition of tolerance had long been practised in the student community and it is still with us. The services were run by the students themselves so that there was always a sense of individual involvement in the prayers and ceremonials. It was not a congregation carried along on the tails of professional leaders. This tradition remains with us to this very day and influences the whole flavour of our service even when, as on this occasion, we have practically no students here.

And so I invite all our friends from Cambridge, from outlying villages of Cambridgeshire, visitors from abroad, especially from Israel and America, to join our service as full participants and share with us its friendliness and informality. Our prayers are expertly led by dedicated members of the community. Come and join us in our prayers in this jubilee year.

Fifty years ago a Jewish State was still a dream. I have recently been reading the personal correspondence of Chaim Weizmann, written between 1914 and 1917 – the publication of the Balfour declaration at the end of that period was like the sudden appearance of a rabbit out of a hat. It was scarcely a viable creature. Jews had chosen other countries of immigration in preference to Palestine (that is why most of us are here rather than there) and yet between 1880 and the outbreak of World War II a modest but persistent stream of Jews from all walks of life established a small but viable community in the Land of Israel. Their efforts and the world situation at the end of World War II opened a unique window in the history of the Jewish people – unique in the sense that it provided, for the first time in two thousand years, an entry into Jewish statehood. Such unique events are cherished and all honour must go to those who pioneered the settlements and development of the country, and to those who followed after the state had been established. Today Israel is thirty-nine years old, beset by intense problems, economic, military, religious and social, but it is a state that by the efforts of its inhabitants and the support of World Jewry is viable and here to stay.

Of course, living as we do in a free democracy we are used to criticizing the government of this country. We complain about unemployment, football hooligans, the unsolved issue of Northern Ireland, the social and economic divide between North and South, the cultural problems of Wales and Scotland, the educational difficulties of the Asian minorities. If I mention these problems it is because they resemble in many ways the problems that Israel faces today. No matter. For all Jews conscious of their history it is a unique privilege to be able to support Israel: it is part of our modest contribution to the Redemption. I hope you will all support the annual United Israel Appeal as generously as you can.

And now to the third part. What shall I say about Yom Kippur itself? I am still under the impact of our synagogue's fiftieth anniversary. But in the history of the Jews it is scarcely more than the twinkle of an eye. The Day of Atonement is an ancient institution well over three thousand years old. It is a serious day but also a festive day and so it was celebrated in ancient times when the Temple still stood.

Today we celebrate it as we have for the last two thousand years as a synagogue service of prayer and supplication. Some distinguished rabbis have held the view that the best place to pray is where you can be alone, undistracted. This scarcely applies to Yom Kippur for two reasons. First, practically all our confessions are in the plural. We do not recite – for the sin *I* have sinned (only the High Priest used that format) – but for the sins that *we* have sinned: it is a collective experience. Secondly, Yom Kippur is an affair of the heart at least as much as an affair of the intellect. The communal melodies, the men dressed in *kittels*, the white *sefer* [*torah*] coverings, the getting up, the sitting down, opening the Ark, closing the Ark, kneeling and prostrating, touch the springs of our hearts. We are moved and it is this condition that gives depth to our prayers. It is in this atmosphere that we are able to respond to our confessions of our past transgressions and that is more than halfway to obtaining forgiveness. As we read the list of *Al Chets* our own conscience will tell us where the sin applies, where the cap fits.

There is an old *midrash* which tells of the power of penitence תשובה. Some time after Cain had been cursed by God for the murder of his brother Abel, his father Adam met him happily working in the field. "How can you be so cheerful," he asked? Cain replied: "I truly repented and God forgave me." Adam responded: "I did not know that repentance could have such power." From this we deduce that Adam did not repent of his sin of eating from the Tree of Knowledge. As we read in Genesis, he blamed it on his wife Hava [Hebrew: Eve]. Hava did not repent either – she blamed it on the serpent. It was Cain who first understood the meaning and power of repentance, of תשובה, the conscious recognition of his own sin and his desire to find absolution. And so he bequeathed to all his descendants, to all mankind, the gift of forgiveness through repentance.

It is for this reason that we are able to pray:

שתסלח לנו על חטאתינו

that the Lord will forgive us for our sins, pardon us for our iniquities and grant remission for all our transgressions. May we all be inscribed in the Book of Life, we and all Thy people of the House of Israel with the blessing of a good life, with peace and with reconciliation. Amen.

I wish you all כתיבה וחתימה טובה [Hebrew: May we all be inscribed and sealed for good in the Book of Life].

Erev Yom Kippur
Thursday 20th September 1988

It is a great honour and privilege for me once more to welcome you all to the Cambridge synagogue to take part in our service: regular members, less regular members, to those from outlying villages and visitors from Israel, from the USA and from other countries. Our services are conducted by our own dedicated members who regard their activities as a *mitzvah* [Hebrew: commandment; colloquially, a good deed] and as a privilege. We shall be expertly led through the service and we hope that you will all take part, not as passengers, but as active participants.

A synagogue, a congregation, a community does need buildings, constitutions, committees, formal organizations. But most of all they depend on people, on individuals who bring their own contribution to the religious, social and intellectual life of the city. In this, Cambridge has been very lucky, and I am pleased to see within the diversity of Cambridge Jewry - and how could there be Jews without diversity - a move towards fuller recognition of the different ways people and groups enrich our communal life.

This year we have seen the departure of active and distinguished stalwarts of the local Jewish life: Lawrence and Nanette Freeman, a family of great piety and scholarship; Violet Lax whose good works have helped numerous individuals and causes - she has gone on *aliyah*; and we shall be losing Ronald and Thelma Domb, who have played such a wonderful and committed role in our religious and communal life; and Lillian and Ivan Roseman who have been so active as a religious and caring family. This is not the place to say how much we shall miss them: we hope they will find what they have gone to seek and that they will come to visit us from time to time. Another member of the Domb family is going on *aliyah* and a young Reif is spending a study year in

Jerusalem. The two main leaders of our service are also going away for a few months. The community will feel all these absences in many ways but I can say with confidence that Cambridge Jewry is strong enough and dedicated and that other members and new members will come forward and play their part in maintaining and enriching the various activities of our communal life. As to our religious involvement, I invite you all to enter actively into the spirit of our service.

It is customary to say a few words about our support for Israel. There is no nation-state that does not have its problems and Israel certainly has its full share. Some of its problems seem to be insoluble - or at least the solutions proposed are mutually incompatible. At present the community is split down the middle over the issue of territories and peace. Those in favour of swapping territories for peace are worried about many things: about timing - is this a good time? - is there even a good time to be conciliatory about security, about the borders, about Jordan and the River Jordan, about frontiers, about international guarantees, whatever they may mean. Those who oppose such a deal simply consider it undesirable and impractical. They see no problem in maintaining the status quo although they do not discuss the long-term demographic and democratic issues involved. There is no easy way and, if it is any consolation, many older states have been unable to resolve some of their longstanding problems.

Jews are renowned for their cleverness in practical affairs, their intellectual achievement, their success in their professions, their devotion to study and learning. Is it possible that we are a people long in scholarship and learning but short in wisdom? Surely this is not so. We must pray that Israel and the Jewish world will show wisdom and resoluteness in carrying out the best decisions that the situation offers.

Allow me to make a point about the media that I made five years ago. We are all conscious of double standards, of the zest with which the media criticize Israel compared to the sullen indifference they show to the massacres occurring on a horrendous scale in neighbouring Muslim countries. The truth is that apart from the columnists who hate the Jews and/or Israel, double standards are practised because they expect Jews to behave better – sometimes they expect us to behave better than they themselves behave. All I can say is: heaven help us and the destiny of Israel and the Jewish people if we come to be judged by the same degraded standards that they take for granted in reporting many other national and international conflicts.

I invite you all to support Israel and the United Appeal in the most generous way you can.

Finally I would like to say a few words about why we are here – about Yom Kippur. I shall not quote some profound observation of a rabbinical sage or Chassidic master. Instead I would like to refer to a simple personal happening that illuminates a much bigger issue.

Last year a relative came to stay with us and one afternoon, while we were entertaining visitors in our garden, he extracted from his luggage a video camera and took some shots of us. Such is the miracle of modern technology that we could each individually look down the viewfinder and play back the shots that had been recorded. It was our first experience and we all lined up for our turn. The interesting feature is that the comments each of us made almost invariably referred to ourselves. One said: "I didn't know that I talked so much with my hands", another: "I didn't realize that my husband looked so much taller then me", another: "My hair falls over my face when I am animated." For my part I noticed that I walked with more of a stoop than seemed sensible and with some effort I have been able to rectify this.

The video revealed a lot about ourselves. Not as we appear in front of a mirror where we primp and beautify ourselves. Not as in a portrait where falseness is frozen for ever. The video showed us as we really are – from the outside.

Yom Kippur is concerned with showing us as we really

are from the inside. That is what the *Al Chets* [communal confession of sins] are telling us. I know that some people rattle through them like firing a machinegun. People must pray as they wish. But it seems to me that all the *Al Chets* are not simply a list of forty-four transgressions that we have necessarily committed in a general sense. I think we are supposed to go through them thoughtfully as though we were scanning our moral failings until we recognize those which really apply to us *individually* through our own *personal experience*. When we come to:

על חטא שחטנו לפניך במשה ובמתן [Hebrew: concerning sins committed in business]

we may recognize that we have actually cheated so-and-so. When we come to:

בלשון הרע [Hebrew: name-calling]

we are not talking about idle tittle-tattle that we all indulge in, but we may recognize and recall so-and-so whom we have made the object of malicious gossip. When we come to: בנטית גרון [Hebrew: arrogance] we are not referring to showing off – which we all do in some measure – we may recall that in speaking to so-and-so we have been intolerably arrogant.

If we want to see how we walk and talk and conduct ourselves among people maybe we should turn to someone to make a video of us when we are not posing. But if we want to get to the meaning of Yom Kippur to see ourselves, as it were, from the inside, let us turn to the *Al Chets* with humility and thoughtfulness. Let us see if we can identify our most serious failings. For if we identify our moral lapses we are halfway to that repentance which Maimonides defined as the remaking of Man's nature in the direction of righteous living. And if we are halfway to repentance then with God's help we may really achieve the full forgiveness that is magnificently expressed in the final triumphal chorus that concludes the *Al Chets*:

ועל כולם אלוה סליחות סלח לנו מחל לנו כפר לנו

[Hebrew: For all of these, O God of Forgiveness, forgive us, be merciful to us, pardon us].

I wish you all כתיבה וחתימה טובה [Hebrew: May we all be inscribed and sealed for good in the Book of Life].

Erev Yom Kippur - Sunday 8ᵗʰ October 1989

[This address was not given: on 7ᵗʰ October, the day before the Kol Nidre service, David was admitted to hospital for by-pass surgery. David had only written the first two paragraphs of the talk.]

Erev Yom Kippur – Friday, 28ᵗʰ September 1990

Last year at this time when we were preparing for Yom Kippur I was suddenly whisked away for an operation which saved my life. And so naturally on this anniversary I have deep emotions and feelings of gratitude to the medical profession and to the *Ribbono shel Olam* [Hebrew: The Master of the World] that today I am here and not there. Last year I had prepared a talk which was aimed mainly at the students, for Yom Kippur was in term and I made nostalgic references to the synagogue in its first years and the changes that have since occurred. All this is now outdated and I must start at the beginning…

[The rest of the talk repeats the talk given in 1986, so it has been omitted.]

Bar- and Bat-Mitzvah Talks:
1967-88

David Tabor

Harvey Ratner Bar Mitzvah
6th May 1967

1. Asked by Chair of local Residents' Committee to say a few words.

2. I wish we had for this a rabbi of scholarship and piety – more appropriate.

3. Nevertheless, since I express the pleasure of all the Jewish residents, visitors, relatives and of the Jewish students here at being present at this *simcha* – the Bar Mitzvah of the oldest son of Dr & Mrs Ratner. Dr Ratner has been a wonderful member of our community. Devoted, loyal, co-operative and tolerant. He has upgraded the Jewish life of this community to an enormous extent. Mrs Ratner has been a tower of strength to him in this work – and in her own right has greatly helped the activities of the Jewish community. We join with them in their *simcha*. It is a wonderful occasion for them – for us. I wish we had more like this.

4. And of course there is the Bar Mitzvah boy himself. Congratulations.

5. Having said this I suppose there is little I can add. You, Harvey, are one of those rare boys in Cambridge who attends synagogue regularly on Saturdays. You have heard all my Bar Mitzvah speeches before, including the old jokes. So I shall not repeat them. Unlike most Jewish boys for whom, as an Anglo-Jewish Rabbi once said, the Bar Mitzvah ceremony is really like a school leaving certificate – for you it is simply one phase of transition in a continuous and continuing line of development as a conscientious and practising Jew. Those of us who have had the problem of bringing up Jewish children in Cambridge, realize what a wonderful achievement this is for your parents as well as for yourself.

May I make one a comment which bears on this week's *sidrah* [Torah portion] which you read so expertly today? It is connected with the Hebrew language which I love and which I know you are studying. This week's *sidrah* is all about Holiness and as you know our rabbis called Hebrew "The Holy Language". You know that the Hebrew word for language is לשון and it is generally treated as a feminine noun. You know that the corresponding Hebrew adjective Holy is קדושה. You may therefore translate "Holy Language" into Hebrew as הלשון הקדושה. But this is not how the Rabbis described it. They described [it] as לשון הקודש – the language of holiness. Hebrew grammarians, of course, will tell you that the construct form לשון הקודש is identical in meaning with the adjectival form הלשון הקודשה. The Hebrew grammarians – may their number increase – may well be right. But I believe that the choice of the rabbinic phrase is no accident of style. I would like to think that in this phrase they really felt that it was the holiness expressed in the Hebrew Language that made it a Holy Language.

Your *sidrah* has probably a more concentrated summary of holiness than any other in the Book of Leviticus. Justice for rich and poor, honesty in weights and measures, rights for the stranger. All these rules are associated with the accompanying phrase – for Jews the Laws they contain are holy. It is the great genius of Judaism that it tries to bring holiness down to earth. Not through abstract religious ideas but through the idea of righteous acts – the *mitzvot* [commandments]. Sometimes...they become rigid, automatic and meaningless, like prayer itself. But every now and again something of the primary impulse breaks through – and in that moment the ritual becomes a living – not a dead – connecting link between the individual Jew and his Maker.

I hope, and I am sure that I speak on behalf of all of us here, residents, visiting relatives, friends and students, that we all wish you health and success in the years ahead, strength and good fortune and happiness and that in the further development of your Jewish personality you will continue to recognize the vital impulse that lies behind all those traditions and rituals that are part of the Jewish way of life. They have, of course, a warmth and beauty of their own but behind [them] stands the specific Jewish idea of holiness, of this relation between man and God.

As a Cohen you now have the privilege on special occasions of pronouncing the priestly benediction on the community. On this occasion of your Bar Mitzvah - I have the privilege of pronouncing it on you.

Present Holy Bible.

Dear Daniel
(No date)

Nothing could give me greater pleasure than to celebrate a Bar Mitzvah here in Cambridge to celebrate the addition of the further member to the adult Jewish community. You were born and educated in America but you are here amongst fellow Jews who rejoice with you on this occasion in your life. Some people talk proudly of the Brotherhood of Man – but brothers often quarrel – I prefer to think today of the phrase *Kol Yisrael Haverim*: we are all friends and support one another. We are all part of a common history, common past and we certainly shall have to stick together to secure a common future.

This is a great day for you and your parents, a great *simcha* in their live and a turning point in yours. You now become a member of a very honourable club – that of the Jewish people – and this means that now you have certain responsibilities. No-one can tell you how much you can, should or must accept of Judaism. But this is so broad a historic and cultural group that there are bound to be areas which you can cultivate and appreciate within Judaism. For although the Fear of God may be the beginning of knowledge, without knowledge your Judaism will be empty and lacking.

Let me just touch on a few of those wonderful rabbinic stories which have been woven around your *sidrah*.

1. When Pharaoh sent the Children of Israel out of Egypt, Moses remarked that the Children of Israel took the jewels and wealth of the Egyptians - but he, Moses, took with him the bones of Joseph. The Children of Israel were concerned with material possessions but Moses knew that without a moral purpose the Exodus would be pointless. All that we know of Joseph indicates that he was a man of high moral standards.

2. The beginning of *sidrah* – [The Children of Israel] shouldn't go near [the] Philistines in case they lost heart. The Rabbis say that Moses led them back so that they shouldn't appear to be running away like escaped prisoners, but leaving in dignity as a people. They stopped at Pi-Hahiroth. According to Rabbinic traditions this was the temple of one of the main Egyptian gods whose statue dominated the surroundings. When the pursuing Egyptians saw the Children of Israel trapped between their main idol and the Red Sea, they were convinced of victory and were keener than ever at the prospect of destroying Israel.

Then Moses began to pray long and hard and God interrupted him and said: "There are times when long prayers are proper and at times when they are out of place. Stop praying and do your stuff."....[Moses] lifted his rod over the waters and commanded the waters to divide. And the waters said: "We were laid down by God; why should we obey what a man tells us?" Then God stood by Moses' side and said: "It is not Moses but I who command you through Moses to divide." At this the waters skipped back and all the waters everywhere divided, and even the water in cups and saucepans divided and remained divided until the Children of Israel had crossed the Red Sea.

Concerning the crossing of the Red Sea the stories are countless, but there is only one that I shall recall. Although the Exodus was the foundation event of the Jewish people and of Judaism and the destruction of Egyptians a crucial episode, it was not to be considered by the rabbis solely as a cause for rejoicing. To this day we omit on the last six days of Passover the recital of those Psalms which recall the drowning of the Egyptian army. Human beings, said God, have been destroyed – do not rejoice even if they are your enemies. This sentiment is part of the religious humanism of the rabbis. At its best it can provide a most ennobling literature for study and contemplation.

Don't pray too much! This also applies to political speeches and sermons.

Bar Mitzvah address to Gary Fox
11 March 1972
ו י ק ה ל - פ ק ו ד י
[Hebrew: vayakhel–pekudei]

First of all I should like to say how delighted we are to be able to celebrate a Bar Mitzvah in Cambridge. This is a very small community and we do not have very many happy occasions. This must be a great *simcha* for your parents, for the community and, of course, for you as the central figure in the whole affair.

You have just read the blessings over a portion of the *sidrah* (in fact a joint *sidrah*) and I would like to make two comments – one to the congregation as a whole – the second to you specifically. This week's *sidrah* is all about the construction and furnishing of the temple in the wilderness during the wanderings of the Children of Israel from Egypt to the Promised Land. When a few hundred years later it was converted into a building of solid stone under Solomon, it was known as the Temple – in its temporary form under Moses it was called the Sanctuary. To most of us nowadays this double *sidrah* is a great bore. The language is exotic, the words and phrases, whether in Hebrew or English, are outlandish and we are never quite sure what they are about even when ingenious men draw what they think it all looked like.

And yet there is something about it that has meaning for us at least at the symbolic level. For in a sense our own personality, our own innermost essence is our own personal sanctuary, our Holy of Holies. There is some core of our being which ultimately determines what we are and what we stand for. And what we learn from this week's *sidrah* is that nothing but the best is good enough to furnish the Sanctuary. The weaving, the tapestry, the curtains, the gold fittings, the lavers, the tongs, the Ark, the seven-branched candelabrum - all these represent the best of what the Children of Israel could provide. So too with the furnishings of our own inner sanctuary, we must strive to provide the best that we can.

But *not* the impossible. There is a wonderful rabbinic legend concerning a discussion between God and Moses when God instructed Moses to build the Sanctuary. Moses said: "But You fill the whole universe, how can I build a sanctuary large enough to match Your majesty?" God replied: "I don't need a sanctuary large enough to match my majesty, I need one that the Children of Israel can build and visit and in it catch a glimpse of Me." When God told Moses about the sacrifices, Moses said: "Sacrifices that match Your honour would need all the Cedars of Hebron for their fires and all the cattle of the Bashan." God replied: "I am not concerned with what I need, I am concerned with what the Children of Israel can provide."

In the Jewish tradition God does not demand the impossible – He asks for the best that is possible.

The furnishings of our inner character demand not the impossible but the best that we can do.

There is one linguistic point that I would like to mention – a button and a flower: *kaftor va ferach*. These were the ornaments on the stems of the seven branches of the candelabrum fashioned by Bezalel. They do not in themselves suggest anything very special but because they were associated with Bezalel's marvellous candelabrum, these words acquired a very special meaning in the Jewish tradition. To this day *kaftor va ferach* means something excellent, wonderful, beautiful, super. And the young Israeli who uses this phrase probably does not realize how it bridges three thousand years and connects modern Israel with the furnishings of the Sanctuary.

And now my second comment is to you, my dear Bar Mitzvah boy. Today you become, as you know, a full member of one of the oldest and most exclusive clubs in the world. It is over three thousand years old – it has had in its time and still has today some most illustrious members. It is the Jewish people. And just as in a good club so in this case membership is not granted lightly. Every member has his duties and responsibilities and each member must fulfil them as best he can. I know how difficult it is in a community so small as Cambridge to find Jewish interests, Jewish friends, Jewish activities that will give some Jewish context to your life. It is a serious problem, but I am sure that your student teacher here and, I hope, your parents will do their best to increase your knowledge of Judaism and to strengthen your involvement in Jewish affairs. I do not know how much Hebrew you know but there is now so much excellent material published in English that no-one can justify ignorance of what Judaism stands for. It is, of course, a challenge. But no-one asks of you the impossible. What one does ask is that you should do the best that you can to fulfil your role as a member of the Jewish community.

Saturday 7th October 1972
Sidrah Bereshit

My dear Bar Mitzvah boy (unnamed)
It is a great pleasure for all of us to join in the joy of your parents and yourself on this happy occasion.

As you know, we have had a surfeit of Jewish festivals during the last month. Exactly a month ago we celebrated the two days of Rosh Hashanah: a week later we had Yom Kippur, but of course that involves a day of preparation and a day – at least – to recover, and then we had a week interrupted by a few ordinary days of Tabernacles. Altogether a very full time – one might say almost too much synagogue – but a Bar Mitzvah is quite different and arouses feelings of happiness and the wish that we could have more of them. For it is a sign of youth taking over and bringing fresh life and activity into Jewish affairs.

This week's *sidrah* is a wonderful poetic account of the Creations of the World, of the first man and woman in it, and of the first hopes and disappointments of mankind. It begins with the phrase, "In the beginning God created Heaven and Earth." There are some who say that this is a poor translation that *bereshit barah* really means "in the beginning of His creation" like *bereshit mamlachto* – so that this first sentence might read better, "When God began to create the heaven and the earth, the earth then being void and without form – He said let there be light." This translation gives the introduction to the Biblical story a more modern ring. Of course, this isn't a new idea. A conservative commentator such as Rashi advances this very explanation himself.

But these attempts to elaborate words or phrases seem beside the point compared with the great underlying ideas of the whole narrative. Placed side by side with all other ancient stories of the creation, the Biblical narrative is outstanding for its simplicity, its clarity and its grandeur. And it is full of direct implications at many, many levels. There is the idea that man is created in God's image. There is the idea that all men are descended from one ancestor and above all there is the initial, basic, optimistic view that the world which God created is good. Every day of creation is good. Indeed on the third day God said it was good twice – and that is why to this day certain Orthodox Jews consider that Tuesday is the proper day on which to enact the marriage ceremony.

The world was good and everything in it. Even man and woman were good until something went wrong and evil entered the world. Adam and Eve sinned. Cain killed Abel and it was Adam's third son Seth who really carried forward the human story.

What do our sages tell us about evil? Their answer is simple or relatively simple. Man has the free choice to make the final decision. However much our sociologists may tell us that everything we do is the result either of heredity or of environment or of both, the final decision is ours – we have enough free will to decide. How then can we have free will if God knows all? If God knows everything how can we have a choice in what we do? Unlike some of our modern rabbis, the ancient rabbis were not frightened to ask such embarrassing questions. I wish our students would follow in the same tradition and ask more questions. The rabbis asked the question and they answered it. God knows all answers and man has got free will to choose between right and wrong. Are these logically incompatible? Yes they are in terms of human reason: and the rabbis frankly admitted it. Any other course would lead to moral fatalism or to a diminution of God's power.

Moral choice and the intrinsic goodness of God's world seem to me to be at least two of the most important ideas that stem from this week's *sidrah*.

To you, my dear Bar Mitzvah boy, I would only like to add the following few words. You have today recited and sung your portion and have become what we call a full member of the Jewish community. It is a good honour because you are becoming part of an ancient people and an ancient culture which has contributed, and may still contribute greatly, to the human scene. Our history of suffering and creativity has given the Jew reason to recall with pride as well as tears the Rock from which he is hewn. It is part of this great tradition that the Jew and every man has within him some part of the majesty of creation, some part of the Divine spark which gives a special quality to his dignity as a man that enables him to distinguish between good and bad, between right and wrong. And many of our traditional *mitzvot* are designed to help us strengthen our spirit in this direction.

I hope you will find the help and encouragement from your friends and teachers and parents to explore the great moral and cultural traditions of our people of which, today, you become a fully responsible member.

Mark Kenneth Freedman
Saturday, 14 October 1972

My dear Bar Mitzvah boy. It is not often that we have such a happy occasion in our community and today marks the second time in two weeks that we have a Bar Mitzvah. It is a great joy to us all to join in this *simcha* and in your parents' *simcha*.

Last week I said a few words to last week's Bar Mitzvah [boy] and I have been asked to say a few words to you today. And I suppose I must first reassure the congregation that they should not worry unduly at the fact that I am again speaking in a synagogue. I am not a rabbi or a son of a rabbi, and this means three things:

1st I cannot speak at length

2nd I cannot take myself too seriously

3rd What I say may not be exactly 120% kosher.

I would like to say a few words about this week's *sidrah*. It is mainly about Noah and the Great Flood. Flood stories appear in many of the legends of the ancients and there are numerous anecdotes concerned with Noah and his Ark. For example, I have a research student from the Soviet Union who comes from Armenia. I asked him about his home town Erevan. He told me it is a beautiful valley surrounded by great mountains. What mountains? The mountains of Ararat. So I asked ноев ковчег? [Russian: Noah's Ark?] Yes, he says, we have a legend that Noah landed on Ararat and planted a vineyard on the slopes of the mountain. Since then Armenians have loved wine!

But the Jewish legend of Noah's wine growing is more illuminating. Noah apparently found the vine which Adam had taken with him from Paradise. It is reported that Satan entered into partnership with Noah in the planting of the vineyard.

Satan slaughtered a lamb, a lion, a pig and a monkey and used the blood of these animals to fertilize the vine. Thus the quality of wine was established for all time. Before man drinks he is as innocent as a lamb; if he drinks moderately he feels strong as a lion, if he drinks more than he can hold he resembles a pig, and if he drinks to the point of intoxication he behaves like a monkey dancing, gibbering and acting obscenely.

Another legend tells of peculiar creatures who found refuge in the Ark. One of these was Falsehood asking for shelter. He was denied admission because Noah only accepted pairs. So Falsehood looked for a partner and found Misfortune and they as a pair were accepted into the Ark. But when they left the Ark, Falsehood found that anything he gathered disappeared into the pockets of Misfortune, and then he realized that though you may gain by falsehood you may lose by misfortune.

One may go on and on, but I think it is time to say a few words of a more serious nature. What moral lesson can we draw from the story of Noah? It seems to me there is a theme which recurs a few times in the Bible and in later history. Noah lived in a sinful society: because he was better than his neighbours the world was saved from complete destruction. In a later event we learn that if there had been ten righteous men in Sodom it would have been saved from destruction and in the more recent tradition based on a comment by Abbaye in the Talmud, it is held that the world is supported by the actions of thirty-six righteous men. The story of Noah reminds us that a good man has an influence far beyond himself and I would like to think that all of us have, potentially, a little bit of Noah in us. All of us have some potentiality within us to help save mankind.

To you, my dear Bar Mitzvah boy, may I say you have sung your portion and today you have become a responsible member of the Jewish community. I do not know how much of this event you will remember in future years, but I suppose one thing you may well recall longer than most other aspects of your Bar Mitzvah, is that it has taken place in a foreign country 3,000 miles away from home, in a strange city and amongst strangers. And yet, of course, we are not strangers, for one of the most remarkable things about our history is that we are all part of one family, of one tradition of our sense of belonging. And today you become a member of this ancient family whose traditions spread back into the beginning of recorded history. Treasure this connection and nourish it, for Judaism provides you with an identity of which you may justly be proud. And remember, too, that like Noah you too have the God-given gift of distinguishing between good and bad and that you have the choice. In your own way, at however modest a level, you can play your part in saving mankind.

I hope that you will find the encouragement of your teachers, parents and friends to strengthen your knowledge of and your participation in those great traditions of our people of which today you become a responsible part.

Bar Mitzvah of Paul Lawrence Bogen 10th November 1973

[Sidrah 'Vayera', the prophetical portion from *Kings*: Elisha and the widow and her son.]

My dear Bar Mitzvah boy. I have been asked to say a few words on this happy occasion and I am very glad to do so. This is a great day in your life and indeed you are the centre of all the celebrations, but there are many others who are happy to share in it. For your parents it is also a great occasion. They have played an increasingly active part in Jewish communal affairs and they have charmed and graced us with their presence. This doubles our [...] joy in their joy. For your relatives, who have come to join in the celebrations, it is also great *simcha* and I wish them a warm welcome to Cambridge. For the Cambridge residents who don't come to synagogue on ordinary Sabbaths – but this is no ordinary Sabbath – it is an occasion for them to share the joy of your parents and family. And for the students who have been so generous of their time and energy in helping you personally and your parents to arrange this celebration, it is also a joyous occasion. Alas, we only collect together in large numbers for funerals and protest meetings. Today we have only good and happy reasons to be together.

It is customary to divide one's words into two parts: one, a commentary on something in the week's *sidrah*, the other as a direct address to you, the Bar Mitzvah boy.

(I improvised some comments about the *Akeda* – the binding of Isaac.)

As to the first part, I cannot really make any useful comments on today's *sidrah*. The story of Abraham's hospitality, his concern for his relatives, his deep faith in God and his overwhelming concern for all those members of his household for whom he felt responsible, all this is so clear

---

and so direct that any commentary would only dilute the effect. Not for nothing was Abraham known as the friend of God and the friend of man. And the *Halftorah* itself, which portrays the piety and simple faith of a simple woman and how her piety and faith finally wins through: it is a perfect narrative and needs no embellishment.

But there is something I would like to say which I think would interest any congregation. It is a comment I heard forty years ago from a visiting preacher on a sentence which occurs at the tail-end of last week's *sidrah* but is really all part of the story we have been reading today, the changing of Sarah's name. You may recall, when God informed Abraham and Sarah that they were to have a son who would be the father of a great nation, He informed them that Sarah's name must be changed. It was originally Sarai – it ended with the Hebrew letter 'Yod' – the 'Yod' must be taken away and replaced by the letter 'He' to give the name Sarah. The simple explanation is that Sarah means princess, whereas Sarai is an old word the meaning of which is not clear. But my visiting preacher produced a very original variant. He made a pun of the Hebrew word for the letter 'yod' or 'yud' and the Yiddish word *jud* or *yid* which means Jew. When God took the 'yud' out of Sarah's name, he said [in Yiddish] עס איז דאָס ערשטע מאָל אַז דער רבונו של עולם העט זיך פאַרצעפעט מיט דאָם ייד. It was the first time God got himself entangled with the Jew, and He has never [since] been able to disentangle himself from the Jew.

I would prefer to invert this and say that this is the first time the Jew got himself entangled with God – and he has never been able to get Him out of his hair. As you know, Jews are like other people only they are different. This difference has been attributed to our peculiar history, our homelessness for two thousand years, our role as perpetual wanderers, as a persecuted minority, as people who always have to try harder than others, etc, etc. But there is one other fact that is at least as important – that tremendous encounter between Abraham and God that took place over three thousand, five hundred years ago. It has left its stamp on the Jewish people for all time. It is an involvement from which we find it very difficult to extricate ourselves, whether we wish to or not.

To you, Paul, today you become a member of a very exclusive club – the Jewish people. Of course we are delighted to welcome you but a club member has responsibilities and duties.

Some people regard the Bar Mitzvah as a *shul*-leaving celebration. I should like to feel that you will regard this as the beginning of a deeper and richer involvement in Jewish learning, Jewish observance, and Jewish understanding. I am sure your parents will give you every encouragement to learn more of the Hebrew language, of the Jewish religion and of its practices – I am sure the students here will help you in the future as they have in the past. I want you to know that you start with all the good will and good wishes of all of us here today in the hope that you will proudly play your part as a member of a people with a proud history, so that your parents, your relatives and friends will be able to say – there goes Paul Bogen, a man who is a credit to his family and to the whole community.

Bar Mitzvah of David Klug
Saturday 17th July 1976

Parashat Pinchas

It is a great honour and a great privilege to be asked to say a few words on this happy occasion, the Bar Mitzvah of the son of our friends the Klugs, and the grandson of a wonderful character, Mr Bobrow. I am sure in other circumstances we would have heard a moving and more authentically Jewish address if Mr Bobrow himself had spoken in my place.

We do not celebrate many *simcha*s in Cambridge and it is a very great pleasure for the community to welcome a new adult member into our fold – after all, it even increases our chances of making a *minyan* [Hebrew: quorum of ten males]. And it must be a source of great joy to David's parents and family to be here today.

I want to say a few words about this week's *sidrah,* and then a few words to the Bar Mitzvah boy himself. This week's *sidrah* contains a mixture of themes – praise for Pinchas and his zeal against idolatry – the rules of inheritance, and finally a whole series of laws concerning sacrifices. The sacrifices described in the *Chumash* [Pentateuch] must surely have seemed essential to our ancestors. They could not have understood religious belief or moral conviction without the rituals of the Sanctuary and the practice of offering sacrifices. But to most of us today the whole issue seems a bore, an exercise for anthropologists and students of comparative religion. Only perhaps in a symbolic way can we extract meaning and meaningfulness from the furnishings of the Sanctuary and the continuous emphasis on sacrifices that involve animals without blemish. For in a sense we all have an inner sanctuary which is our own Holy of Holies, and the attributes that we bring to it determine an innermost character and the qualities that make up our own personalities. It is surely no coincidence that the Hebrew word for 'without blemish' תמים also conveys the idea of perfection, of uprightness and of integrity. These provisions for the Sanctuary are as important to the individual as their animal forms were to the sacrifices of our ancestors.

Judaism makes moral demands on us all but it does not ask for the impossible. There is a wonderful rabbinic legend concerning a discussion between God and Moses concerning the Sanctuary and the sacrifices. When God instructed Moses to build the sanctuary Moses said: "Lord of the Universe, You fill the whole Universe – how can I build a house large enough to match Your majesty?" God replied: "I don't need a Sanctuary large enough to match my majesty – I need only a house that the Children of Israel can build and visit and in it catch a glimpse of my majesty." When God told Moses about the sacrifices, Moses said: "Sacrifices that would match Your honour would need all the cedars of Lebanon and all the cattle of the Bashan." God replied: "I am not concerned with what I need, I am concerned with what the Children of Israel can provide." In the Jewish tradition, it is not the impossible that is asked for: it is the best that is possible. The inner chambers of our personality demand not impossible sacrifices but the best that we can do. And it is this inner quality of our own personality that responds to the call of the small, quiet voice which Elijah describes in the *Haftorah* which we would have read this week - the quiet voice of conscience that speaks of integrity, honesty, uprightness and, as I am sure Mr Bobrow would have emphasized, of social justice.

And now I would like to say a few words to the Bar Mitzvah boy himself. Today you have become a full member of one of the oldest and most exclusive clubs in the world. It is over three thousand, five hundred years old: it has had in its time, and it still has today, some extremely illustrious members. It is the Jewish people. From the time of Abraham, whose encounter with God has left its stamp on the Jewish people for all time to this very day, the Jews have been different. And even in their attempts to normalize their life in

Israel, they still remain in some ways, even in the process of normalization, a nation apart. This peculiar quality of the Jewish people is reflected in the beautiful imagery of this week's *Haftorah*.

Of course, as in all good clubs, so in joining the club of the Jewish people, membership demands duties and responsibilities and most of all it demands an understanding of the history, the religious ideas and the social ideals which make up its constitution. There is now so much excellent material available in English that no-one can nowadays justify ignorance of what Judaism stands for. I know that in a small community like Cambridge it is not easy to find Jewish interests, friends and activities that will give Jewish content and Jewish purpose to your life. It is a serious challenge but no-one asks of you the impossible. What one does ask is that you do your best to fulfil your role as a member of the Jewish community. I am sure you will get the maximum help and support from your parents, from your brother, from your grandfather and from your other relatives; and you carry with you the best wishes of the whole of the community in this first stage of your entry into the fold of the Jewish people.

Sunday 25ᵗʰ July 1976
Bat Mitzvah of Ariela Morag
בת-מצוה אריאלה מורג

M y dear Ariela,
Your parents have asked me to say a few words and I really do not know what they expected me to say. If it was Torah or Hebraica, I am sure your father would do better; if it was wise advice, I am sure your mother would do better, and if it was just to hear a sweet voice, you would do better than all of us.

This is a very happy day in your life and a day of great happiness for your parents, your family and friends. You are also a very lucky girl: for you not only have a very happy home life but you are one of that new generation of Jews or Jewesses who for the first time in nearly two thousand years have the privilege of being born free.

I am only sorry that you could not be Bat Mitzvah in the Synagogue - but I'm afraid Rabbinic Judaism at present does not permit it. Perhaps in two thousand years time it will have found some formula that will make it possible. I am sure that if Rabbi Hillel were alive today he could and would do something about it, but probably he would be excommunicated (put in *cherem*) by the *Neturai Karta* or maybe even by the Lubavitchers. I do, of course, recognize the difficulties. Imagine having to rewrite the prophets (the *Sefer Neviim*) and instead of saying ואתה בן אדם [Hebrew: and you, son of Adam] having to say ואת בת חוה: [Hebrew: and you, daughter of Eve].

So we are having it here on a Cambridge College lawn on a typical summer afternoon, amidst friends and well-wishers in the shadow of the Pythagoras building. And it struck me that this very building can be used as a measuring rod, for you see, it is over seven hundred years old. When it was built the great centres of Jewish life were not in Eastern Europe, certainly not in America. They were in France, in Germany, in Spain and especially in North Africa and the Arab countries. Maimonides was a young man. There were even Jews in Cambridge at that time – not many, but some until they were all expelled by King Edward just over seven hundred years ago. We had to wait four hundred years before Jews began to trickle back into this country.

Seven hundred years is a long time. Seven hundred years ago the great Jewish communities were worried by the Crusades and worried for different reasons about the impact of philosophy on religion. And seven hundred years before that there were practically no Jews in Spain and Western Europe. The great centre was Babylon where the Ge'onim were finishing the Talmud, the crown of rabbinic Judaism. And seven hundred years before that the most important centre for the future of the Jewish people was in Eastern Israel itself for that was the period of the Maccabean revolt and the renewed independence of the Jewish state.

It was also the time when our great rabbis developed those ideas which enabled Judaism to survive without the Temple service.

And seven hundred years before that we come to more or less the beginning of the great prophetic tradition started by Amos and Hosiah, whose words still have the power to move our hearts and minds.

Have I finished yet? No, I have not. Seven hundred years before that we come to the time when the Children of Israel were wandering herdsmen, or perhaps slaves in Egypt awaiting their liberation by Moses, the leader and teacher of the Jewish people And still we have to go back several more hundreds of years before we come to Abraham, who started it all. For it was Abraham's encounter with God, his religious vision which he passed on to his descendants, which turned us from nomads and peasants into an Eternal People, an עם עולם. This vision of Abraham's has set its stamp on us for all time so that, willingly or unwillingly, we cannot free ourselves from it. As Bialik once wrote concerning the committed, sensitive Jew, he is the faithful guardian of God's form on Earth [אתם השומרים בנאמנים לצלם אלהים בעולם]. And it is in this people which you are entering today, this people which even in trying to normalize its life in Israel, still remains a peculiar people, an עם סגולה.

Let me just add one thought. Abraham saw the real hard world around him – the world of material things, of facts, of action. He also saw a world of ideas, ideals, visions: a spiritual world. There is always a tension between them. And it is the genius of rabbinic Judaism that it took these ideas from the world of the spirit and converted them into concrete practices. It brought them into the world of action so that these ideas became part of the real world around us. That is what the rabbinic idea of the *mitzvot* is all about. It turns ideas which are difficult to grasp into actions which we can all carry out if we have the will to do so.

I know, and it is all part of the traditional home in which you have been brought up, that you will always remain attached to the warmth and sense of stability which the *mitzvot* provide. But it may be [that] when you are a little older you will begin to ask yourself once again questions about those ideas, ideals and visions, those basic religious beliefs on which all our traditions and ceremonials are based. And then you will need to find a way, which every individual has to find for himself and for herself, how to bring these two worlds [the secular and the religious] into harmony...

In this challenging task you may get help from your family and your teachers. But most of all the answer will come, if there *is* an answer, from your own lifestyle and from the lifestyle of those who form part of your own circle. In this great task I wish you חזק ואמץ or maybe חזקי ואמצי [Hebrew: be strong and of good courage (first in the masculine and then in the feminine forms)].

Bar Mitzvah David Lask
7th October 1977
Shabbat Bereshit

May I say how happy I am to see such a full synagogue, and to welcome all those visitors as well as our students who have come to today's service.

Your parents have asked me to say a few words on this occasion of your Bar Mitzvah and I am very glad to do so. This is a very happy occasion and a great *simcha* for all of us, for the community, for the family and for you personally.

For the community, because it makes the entry of one more member into its fold. You now count as a fully-fledged member of the Jewish congregation. It is marvellous for us to add to our members. And all those in this full synagogue show how many of our members share in this joy.

For your family, because it is a special occasion for many reasons. I have been acquainted with your mother's family for the last forty years and I well remember your grandparents living in Fitzroy [Street] before the war. At that time there were only six Jewish families in Cambridge and I believe your Uncle Clive – your mother's brother – was the first Jewish boy to be born in Cambridge for about a hundred years. That community was a very small one, and it faced the terribly difficult problem of maintaining Jewish interests and Jewish loyalties amongst its children. It is a great tribute to your grandparents that they succeeded in this task and that your mother and your father have been able to maintain a Jewish home and a happy and creative Jewish atmosphere. Your grandparents would have been delighted to see that in you, the third generation has been able to continue the tradition.

You have acquitted yourself excellently and for you this is a special day, for today you enter into one of the most exclusive clubs in the world – that of the Jewish people. It carries with it great privileges and great responsibilities, but it is a very distinguished club and the membership fee is well worth paying.

What can I say about this week's *sidrah* itself? It is a magnificent picture of the creation of the universe and stands head and shoulders above all the ancient cosmologies by its directness, simplicity and uncompromising monotheistic approach. I do not wish to discuss the question of creation from nothing – a theme ingeniously tackled by Maimonides eight hundred years ago – nor do I wish to raise the whole question of the story of *Bereshit* [Genesis] in relation to modern science. Such discussions have their place but this is not the time to raise them.

Instead, I would like to mention two themes which seem to me to be worth commenting about. First, all the acts of creation are described in the language "and God said: 'Let there be...'" light in the firmament, water, earth, plants, animals, fish, birds. Only of man does it say – and God made man – made him in His own likeness. Man was the pinnacle of creation, and by virtue of this he possesses some part of the Divine Spark, some element that enables him to respond to the religious emotion, to worship and to pray. We saw something of this three days ago on *Simchat Torah* [Rejoicing of the Law]. There is - or there could be if we look hard enough - a bit of God in all of us.

The second theme concerns the Tree of Knowledge. For ever since we partook of the fruit of this tree, we have been blessed – or cursed - with the irrepressible urge to ask questions. To ask questions is to use our intellectual faculties and to exercise one of the gifts that distinguishes man from the animal kingdom. I know that some religious figures believe that we should not ask questions for fear we get the wrong answer. Others, that we should not ask questions because our intellect is limited – which is true – and that our intellect cannot cope with all problems. Others that we should not ask religious questions because they are irrelevant

– the main thing is to observe the *mitzvot* and not to reason why.

All these excuses seem to me to miss the point concerning religion at its best and most creative - the tension between faith and doubt, the tension between what we think we believe and what we really believe – for, in the long run, if we run away from this issue we are incomplete men – religiously and morally.

This contrast should have been brought home to us last week when we were supposed to recite the Book of Ecclesiastes. This exciting book, full of self-criticism, full of doubt, full of questioning, full of pessimism, was believed by some of our ancient rabbis to be so heretical that they considered it should not be included in the Bible. (Some of those rabbis have descendants in our present Bet Din.) But the book was included, just as the even greater Book of Job was included, because ultimately the rabbis of old were strong enough in their faith. They were fully committed to the observance of the *mitzvot* but they were not frightened men. Their faith was strong enough to be strengthened by honest and perceptive questioning.

Of course, Judaism has invented an approach to religious belief which is something more than simple faith and abstract theory. It is the principle of religious observance which provides the background for our beliefs and our religious commitment. The *mitzvot* do provide the moral and emotional framework on which we can build our intellectual and critical understanding of what Judaism is about. It is an amalgam in which faith and doubt, practice and criticism, private and public worship are essential ingredients.

To you, my dear Bar Mitzvah boy, I can only say this. You now live in a community which provides you with Jewish friends, Jewish youth activities and Jewish educational opportunities which were not here forty years ago. You have the encouragement of your parents and family and the Jewish community…You have it in your own hands to face up to the challenge of becoming an active and creative member of the House of Israel. The task of carrying on the Jewish tradition was faithfully transmitted by your grandparents to your parents. Your parents, themselves active in Jewish life in Cambridge, now pass it on to you. If you will set aside some time for Jewish study, for Jewish observance [and] for Jewish interests, we are sure you will not fail to become another vital link in our heritage.

Let me conclude with a fragment from an old prayer: "Put understanding into my heart that I may comprehend wisely and fulfil all the words of the study of the Law in all its depth. Deliver me from error and purify my thoughts and my heart for Your worship."

We all wish you every success in this Great Task חזק ואמץ [Hebrew: be strong and of great courage].

Dinner for [the] Bar Mitzvah of Aryeh Reif, St John's College 12ᵗʰ June 1983, 7.30pm

R eply to toast to the guests by Mr Stekel (Shuli Reif's father).

(This was the last of several speeches – by then it was about 10pm, and although Stekel's talk was very well worked out, enough was enough. I tried to shorten mine, particularly as everything that could be said seemed to have been said already.)

It is a great honour and pleasure to be asked to respond on behalf of the guests to the toast and I am sure I am expressing their feelings when I say how delighted we are to be here.

Those of us who have had the experience of bringing up Jewish children in Cambridge know what an achievement it has been to educate Aryeh and Tania in Judaica so effectively. And this has been more than an educational achievement – for they have acquired not only knowledge but joy in their Judaism and a zest for participating fully in all aspects of Jewish life.

It is, of course, a tribute to Shuli and Stefan Reif which all of us recognize, and they must be extremely proud and happy on this occasion. We share this happiness – indeed I will invent a word to describe our feeling: *Freudenfreude* – the joy in other people's happiness. But perhaps in these august surroundings it might be more appropriate to express it in Yiddish and to say how glad we are to see all the Reif generations: *Wie see Kleiben Nachas fun die Kinder, eniklich in ureniklach.*

All the previous speakers have spoken of the fact that in looking at Aryeh (and Tania) one really sees the influence and character of their parents. I am reminded of that Yiddish proverb which says:

Der eppel falt nisht veit fun baum

The apple doesn't fall far from the tree of which it is the fruit.

And here we see the fruit in Aryeh and Tania, and the tree from which they have a sprung – Shuli and Stefan – and the tree from which Shuli and Stefan have sprung (all grandparents now) and the tree from which they themselves derive (there is one great-grandmother happily here). And so we can go back over the generations to some primal tree some *Urbaum* with which it all started.

It was a strong and sturdy tree, able to withstand storm and tempest, flood and drought, marauding gangs and hostile climates. And in each generation it has produced its fruit which in due course has produced another tree, equally sturdy and robust. So it has gone on, generation after generation, until we see it here before our eyes, vigorous and flourishing, secure in its future.

It is, of course, the Tree of Life.

Adam Squires' Bar Mitzvah
Saturday 23rd May 1987

Introductory phrases in Hebrew:

ראשית כל רוצה אני להדיע קבלת פנים חמה לדודא ולסבה
ולסבתה שנסעו כאן מישראל ובאו בכדי לחוג אתך את
היום המיוחד הזה, יום שבו אתה נכנס לבית ישראל.

בית ישראל הוא בית עתיק-יומין, עומד ונוסד על יסודות חזקים
ובריאים, יסודות של אמונה, מצוות, למוד, חבות בין אדם
לחבירו, וכולי.

כולנו פו היום חברים ותיקים של הבית ומברכים אותך ומקבלים
אותך כחבר חדש בחיבה ובשמחה. חזק!

עכשיו אתה בינינו כבן הבית.

[First of all I want to give a warm welcome to your aunt
and to the grandparents who have travelled from Israel
specially to celebrate with you on this special day, the day on
which you enter the community of Israel. The House of
Israel is ancient; it stands on firm and healthy foundations of
faith, commandments, learning, the duties between man and
his fellow man, and so on. We here are all old friends of this
House and we welcome you and receive you as a new friend
and member with love and joy. Be strong! Now you are
sitting with us as a son of the house.]

My dear Adam,

I suppose you must be wondering at the coincidence that
your auntie and your grandparents have come from the State
of Israel to celebrate with you your entry into the House of
Israel. It is no coincidence – the State of Israel, the Land of
Israel, the House of Israel are all part of the unfolding history
of our people.

The House of Israel is very old, very venerable, but it is
still full of life. It is based on very strong, healthy and rugged

foundations – foundations of belief, commandments, learning, duties of man to his neighbour, duties of man to God. All these are expressed in the portions of the Torah which you have read from so excellently today. There is God speaking directly to Moses in the first verse of *BeHar*: this is the God of our belief. There is the last verse of your *Haftorah* – These are the commandments which the Lord commanded Moses for the Children of Israel. There is throughout the Torah the understanding that we are to study it. It is our life and the length of our days. It can, of course, take many forms. Your *sidrah* deals with the Jubilee when the Land was made free for people to repossess – it is concerned with the duties of man to his neighbour – his social responsibilities. Thus belief, *mitzvot*, learning, responsibility to society are fundamentals. It is not possible for me to say which, if any, of these is the most important.

But it seems to me that with all the experiences the Jewish people have been through, the House of Israel has grown into a very broad and spacious House. And anyone who enters it with love and respect will be able to find in it some corner, some room where he can apply his talents to reinforce the foundations, strengthen the walls and beautify the contents.

There are many academics in Cambridge who have left the House of Israel. It is our loss – it is also theirs. Your parents have shown how it is possible to be involved in the professional life of Cambridge and yet still remain committed Jews and active in the community. They are an example you can be proud of, and I am sure that you will find your way of doing likewise.

All of us here are old members of the House of Israel – today you become a new fully-fledged member. All of us here congratulate you and welcome you and wish you well.

There is just one other point. You are a Cohen and now that you are Bar Mitzvah you have the privilege and the duty of blessing the congregation on those occasions when ברכת הכוהנים [Hebrew: the Priestly Blessing] is recited. But today

I would like to reverse the procedure. All the congregation here, I am sure, will join me in praying that the Lord will bless and keep you, that He will shine upon you and be gracious to you, that He will favour you and grant you Peace.

Adam Raymond's Bar Mitzvah
Saturday 23rd April 1988

I t is a great pleasure for me to welcome to this synagogue all those who have come here to celebrate Adam's Bar Mitzvah. Grandparents, parents, uncles and aunts, cousins and friends. We are glad to see you and we rejoice with you in the *simcha* that has brought you here. A Bar Mitzvah is a great occasion for you who have come, it is a great occasion for the Jewish community of Cambridge and it is especially a unique occasion for Adam himself. As I mentioned to him last week, you only get Bar Mitzvah'd once in your life, though I must warn Adam that when he reaches the age of 83, that is the 70th anniversary of the present occasion, he may be expected to celebrate it in a very special way as a sort of second Bar Mitzvah. So it is something to look forward to.

Adam, in reaching your Bar Mitzvah you enter one of the oldest and most exclusive and distinguished clubs in the world: you become a fully-fledged member of the House of Israel. This House is very old, very venerable but still full of life. It is built on very strong, healthy and rugged foundations – foundations of belief, commandments, learning, duties of man to his neighbour, duties of man to God. I know that you have been studying with Daniel Michaels and with Julian Landy, and I am sure that if you will continue you will become better acquainted with the basic principles of Judaism in which belief and practice, study and prayer and responsibility to society are fundamentals. It is not possible for me to say which, if any of these is the most important. At various times, in various places and in various situations, experts have expressed opinions on this. I am no expert.

But it seems to me that with all the experiences the Jewish people have been through during the last three thousand years, the House of Israel has grown into a very broad and spacious House. Anyone who enters it with affection and respect will be able to find in it some corner, some room where he can apply his talents and his interests to reinforce the foundations, to strengthen the walls and to beautify the contents.

You live in a rather isolated part of the countryside, but I do hope you will be able to come to Cambridge and take part in some of the activities which the community and the students can provide. You will find here not only the opportunity to take part in Jewish services and Jewish study but also in youth activities such as Bnei Akiva, Habonim or Noar Zioni. You will find young Jews nearer your own age, and in particular during term-time, you will find students who play such an active part in Jewish life in Cambridge anxious and willing to help you find your place as a committed member of the House of Israel.

All of us here are old members of the House of Israel – today you are our newest recruit and we all welcome you and congratulate you and wish you well.

We wish you good fortune מזל טוב

I am sure that all the congregation here will join me in praying that the Lord will bless you and keep you, that He will shine upon you and be gracious to you, that He will favour you and give you peace.

On behalf of the Jewish community here I am very happy to present you with this copy of the Pentateuch – the Five Books of Moses – for their message is our life and the length of our days.

Poems, talks and articles:
a selection

David Tabor

Witnesses

(Heretical thoughts after the High Holy Days)
The tempter said: "The Tree of Life is dead.
   There is no God and you are his witnesses."
If this cruel paradox be true
He must be laughing up his sleeve
  At all our prayers, our pleas and supplications
uttered and muttered,
declaimed and proclaimed from well-worn texts
amid rich rites and fervent ceremonial;
chanted and chorused in public ecstasy
with passion fit to thaw the cosmic void
and melt a path into his vacant chamber.
I think he must find us rather odd
      and very small
and in his non-existent way
be telling us not to pray
or not to pray so much
or not to pray at all –
      but to listen more.
We listened well, once, long ago.
The lightning flashed,
  the mountain shook with fire and smoke
and through the booming thunder, the roaring flames
  the howling tumult of the troubled elements
We heard each word, distinct, unblurred – but now
Only the soundless echo
  flicks and riffles through the yellowing leaves
The book is silent
  and the tree is bare.
Will buds renew?

(1988, unpublished)

Chaloymes
[Yiddish: 'Dreams']

MOTHER   My mother, of blessed memory
          Lived to be ninety-four.
          When infirmity and the burden of years
          Proved specially irksome
          And old-age seemed deprived of every joy
          She would quote the apt old Russian adage:
           "*Starost 'nye radost*" – [Old age is no joy]
          When he came home we would all sit
          Round a huge circular table for we were a large
               family
          Seeking comfort in the rhyme and rhythm
          Of the verbal diptych.
          But in her later years she would
          Muse more often
          On the insubstantiality of past events
          The transience of life, its unreality.
          Then she would relapse into her folksy Yiddish
          And say, speaking from long experience,
          "*Dos Leben iz a Cholem.*" [Life is a dream]

FATHER   My father worked hard all his life
          At first six days a week, later five
          He would leave early in the morning and return
               after seven.
          (We had already eaten our tea, brown bread and
               butter and
          Watercress, and begun our homework to the
               music of Jack Payne).
          When he came home we would all sit
           round a huge circular table, for we were a large
               family
           and eat our evening meal with undiminished
               appetite.

The table would be cleared, perhaps by my
    sisters.
My mother would sit quietly sewing or playing
    Patience,
while we would talk and tease one another
 or finish off our homework.
My father would take the only armchair by the
    fire
and read the evening paper –
And while reading, relax and fall asleep – his
    head on one side.
Often he would snore until some final climactic
    rattle would
wake him;
He would look at us with open innocent eyes
As though he were seeing us for the first time
    and ask perplexedly:
"*Hob ich takeh geshlofn?*" [Was I really asleep?]
We had heard the question many times before.
"No", we would reply rather naughtily,
"you did not sleep – you dreamt it."
It was our customary answer –
"*Du host es gecholemt.*"

(Published in the *CJRA Newsletter*, New Year/September
1990, p.15.)

Ahad Ha'am and Mendele:

An anecdote by D Tabor

M endel Mocher S'forim, the pen-name of Shalom Jacob
Abramowitsch (1835-1917), is widely regarded as the
grandfather of modern Yiddish. He used the language as a
vehicle for a secular literature introducing both satire and
affection unto his descriptions of contemporary Jewish life in
Eastern Europe. He was a great innovator and a shrewd
spectator of men and affairs. (One has only to compare *Die
Kliyatshe* with Sholem Aleichem's *Rapchik* to gauge the gap
between the master and the apprentice.) In later years he
turned once again to Hebrew and developed a style that had a
seminal influence on post-Haskala [Jewish Enlightenment of
the 19th century] literature. Except for a three-year residence
in Geneva (1905-1907) he spent the last thirty-six years of his
life in Odessa.

Odessa was a great centre of Jewish literary and political
activity. His contemporaries there included famous Hebrew
and Yiddish writers, secular historians, Talmudic scholars,
Zionists and Bundists. Mendele conducted what might well
be called a literary salon. No doubt modern Yiddishists would
be tempted to call it a *Kulturele un Literarische Gezelshaft* but in
fact it was affectionately known as Mendele's Cheder. To this
circle came many distinguished figures to discuss life and
literature.

In the year 1904, Ahad Ha'am completed one of his best
known essays; it deals with Moses. In this work he suggests
that the Moses we venerate in the Pentateuch is not a man of
flesh-and-blood, or at least not necessarily a man of flesh-
and-blood. He is essentially a projection of the Jewish
National Image of an ideal. He is not the ideal leader,
legislator, statesman or magician: he is the ideal prophet. It is
in these terms that Ahad Ha'am develops once again his
concept of a secular Jewish ethic. The essay is full of passion,

powerfully argued and resonates with the author's devotion to a cultural Hebraic Nationalism.

When he had finished reading his paper to the assembled circle of friends there was a hushed silence. Mendele arose in great anger and spoke. "According to our holy scriptures," he said, "we are told that Moses died and was buried and no-one knows his burial place unto this very day." And then he added a devastating and trenchant comment: "*Ot do hot ihr ihm bagroben.*" Right here and now you have buried him.

Of course, we may read Ahad Ha'am's essay with a sounder perspective and understand better the various factors that influenced his outlook. We still do not know where Moses is buried but his Torah still lives on in our hearts and minds.

When I was told this story in 1939 I knew of no published book in which it was recorded. In accordance with ancient rabbinic tradition it is proper for me to give my source. At the beginning of World War II the London School of Oriental Studies was evacuated to Cambridge where I was then a research student. I enrolled in a course of Modern Hebrew under Isidore Wartski, Ahad Ha'am Lecturer in Modern Hebrew. We studied Bialik, Ahad Ha'am and best of all, the biblical book of the prophet Amos. It was while we were reading some extracts from Ahad Ha'am's writings – it may have been from the essay on Moses himself – that Isidore Wartski told us this story of how Ahad Ha'am was deemed to have buried Moshe Rabbenu ['Moses our Teacher'] in Mendele's Cheder in Odessa eighty years ago.

(Published in *The Jewish Chronicle* Literary Supplement, 15 June 1984, p.vii.)

Deborah – The First Rheologist?

W hat is rheology and what has it to do with Deborah, prophetess and mother–in–Israel, for whom the stars in their courses fought to vanquish Siserah? We know of Deborah; what do we know of rheology?

Rheology is the scientific study of the flow of materials, whether they are gasses, liquids or solids. The word is derived from the Greek word *rheos*, but there are not many familiar words in English which employ this root word. Those that do are mostly unpleasant, like diarrhoea (*nicht bei uns gedacht!*). There are many factors involved in the flow behaviour of materials. Two of them involve time. One is the time for which the force or stress is applied. The longer the time, the more the flow that is produced. The other is the time that the material takes to 'relax' from the effect of flow once the force is removed. The shorter the 'relaxation' time, the more easily the material flows. For example, with water the relaxation time is less than one millionth of a millionth of a second. Consequently, we need to apply a force for only a very short interval of time to produce appreciable flow. With oil the relaxation time is a thousand times longer. We have to apply the force a thousand times longer to produce the same flow as in water. For pitch, the relaxation time is a day or so. But the largest relaxation times are those associated with the flow of rocks – hundreds of thousands or millions of years. This means that if rocks are to flow, enormous periods of time must elapse. And this is where Deborah comes in.

In her famous victory hymn recording the discomfiture of Siserah on the slopes of Mount Tabor, his final defeat by Barak and his death at the hands of Jael, she sings triumphantly of the sovereignty of the Lord, creator and ruler of the Earth. As a tribute to his power, she recites: "Harim nazlu mipneh haShem" – "The mountains flowed before the Lord." As Professor Reiner pointed out: "In God's time, even the mountains will flow," and this has been substantiated in all the latest studies of the flow of the Earth's crust. The continents as we know them today have arrived at their present shape as a result of millions of years of flow (I refer here, of course, to geological time – not biblical time).

It was Professor Reiner who first raised this matter and its implications. Marcus Reiner, a kibbutznik with a deep love of the Bible and a Professor at the Haifa Technion, was a world authority on rheology. At an International Conference of Rheologists held over twenty years ago he proposed that the ratio of the relaxation time to the force time should be given a name and that it should be called the Deborah number. As a tribute to Professor Reiner himself, and in recognition of the poetic justice of the suggestion, it was accepted with acclaim. And ever since, rheologists all over the world, atheists in the Soviet Union, Buddhists in China, Hindus in India, Shintoists in Japan, or Moslems in Arabia, refer to this ratio as the Deborah number.

There is, of course, a mystical dimension to this. According to some Cabbalists and mystics, in the messianic age the existing biblical prohibitions will no longer apply, for man will no longer need them. A new bible will replace the old. Is it then possible that the epic story of Deborah will vanish? In that case her name will live on, not in holy scriptures, not in the scholarly insights of the rabbis, but in the words and writings of engineers, mathematicians and rheologists engaged in the study of flow. In this way, unwittingly perhaps, they will perpetuate for all time the name of this heroic leader of an ancient people.

(Talk first given in the synagogue at Thompson's Lane, January 1986.)

The Rabbi and the Journalist

The last contact between Chief Rabbi Hertz and Nahum Sokolow

This year [1986] marks the fortieth anniversary of the death of Rabbi Hertz and the fiftieth anniversary of the death of Nahum Sokolow.

Chief Rabbi Hertz

J oseph Herman Hertz was born in Slovakia in 1872 and received his secular and rabbinic education in New York. He was serving as a rabbi in Johannesburg when the Boer War broke out in 1899 and was expelled by President Kruger because of his pro-British sympathies. After the British victory, he was reinstated and was viewed with considerable favour by the British authorities. In 1913 he was called to serve as Chief Rabbi if the 'United Hebrew Congregations of the British Empire', succeeding Hermann Adler. He spent the rest of his life in that position and travelled widely, visiting Jewish communities in the Commonwealth and other parts of the world.

Hertz was a strong and forceful character, and to those of my generation who grew up between the Wars he was viewed with respect, a little fear, and a certain amount of quizzical affection. This was partly because of his characteristic accent, intonation and mannerism, as well as his gift for pithy aphorisms, all of which invited imitation. Indeed, almost every student and youth entertainment would include a sketch in which he was impersonated.

There were three aspects of his activities which left a particularly strong impression on me. The first was his little *Book of Jewish Thoughts*, which was something new for Anglo-Jewish readers, and is still worthwhile reading although published over sixty years ago. The second was his commentary on the Pentateuch and *Haphtorahs*, which was a milestone in Anglo-Jewish literature. It provided for the first time a readable, intelligent, and sometimes (not always intentionally) entertaining text to retain the interest of congregants lost in the *sidrah* or bored with the surrounding gossip. Although on important issues the conclusions always ended on the orthodox side of the fence, Hertz was open and forthright in discussing contentious issues such as evolution, the authorship of the Pentateuch, [and] the Temple sacrifices. There was a certain breadth about his orthodoxy. This was shown in the struggle he experienced in maintaining a middle course in Anglo-Jewish affairs. At one point, when he was being pushed to denounce those who supported a less rigid form of observance, he observed: "Our problem today is not religious difference but religious indifference." There was wisdom as well as courage in that remark, and it is the third aspect of his work that I remember.

Hertz was a keen defender of Jewish rights, and a staunch Zionist. His death in 1946 robbed Anglo-Jewry of an outstanding religious and communal leader.

Nahum Sokolow

Nahum Sokolow was known as the father of Hebrew journalism. He was born in Poland in 1860 of a long line of rabbinic scholars. He was an *ilui* (child prodigy), and was fully saturated with Bible, Talmud and Hebrew learning. He never attended a secular school or university, but his keen and absorbent intellect enabled him to enter into numerous fields of learning and scholarship. At an early age he began to write for the Hebrew press of his day and soon became known for his essays and literary articles.

Because of the ease with which he absorbed knowledge and used it there were many stories about his gifts. It was said that he could write the libretto for an opera, compose the music, conduct the orchestra and sing the main roles! When he was editor of the official Hebrew journal of the Zionist movement, *HaOlam* [The World], he wrote an editorial in Aramaic suggesting that in a future Jewish state, Hebrew might be considered too holy for mundane affairs. He was in

David Tabor

London with Weizmann in World War I and undertook a number of diplomatic missions of great importance. There was a quiet dignity and urbanity in his manner which fitted him for this task, and he was able to obtain approval of the Balfour Declaration from the French, Italian, Rumanian and South African governments. He visited the Pope in 1917, and was accorded a sympathetic reception. This led to the Eastern European Jewish joke that when Sokolow and the Pope supposedly appeared at the balcony of the pontifical building, the crowd called out: "Who is that man standing next to Nahum Sokolow?"

He was a man of calm dignity and studied impartiality, and avoided controversy. In 1931, when Weizmann resigned from the presidency of the World Zionist Organization, Sokolow took his place until Weizmann returned in 1935. Sokolow wrote countless articles, essays and feuilletons in numerous languages and a number of books. Two of these made a strong impression on me. The first was a two-volume work in English on the early history of Zionism. Apparently Manchester University accepted his *yeshivah* qualifications as equivalent to a first degree, and allowed him to register as an external student for the PhD. The two-volume history was the result and it contains an incredible record of forgotten authors and essays in many languages, covering mainly the early part of the nineteenth century. He obtained his doctorate!

The second is his Hebrew book on *Spinoza and his times.* It greatly impressed me with its vigour and modernity of approach. Yet, in some ways, Sokolow was still part of an older generation. I remember hearing him lecture (around 1934) on new developments in Hebrew language and literature. He expressed the hope that the whole of world literature would become accessible to the Hebrew reader, but surprised me by saying that he was not sure if he would approve of a Hebrew translation of *The Decameron.* When I read that work for the first time a decade or more later, I recalled his comment and understood it, but by that time tastes had changed and I have no doubt his own view would have been different.

In 1936 he took a few Spanish lessons to brush up his knowledge of the language before embarking on a propaganda and fund-raising tour of South Africa. He was in his seventy-sixth year, and in the midst of his preparations collapsed and died. I was amongst the group of young Zionists who stayed on guard by his bedside (as a 'watcher') before he was taken away for burial. His funeral was attended by a vast assembly of Jews from all walks of life and the service was conducted by Chief Rabbi Hertz. I remember that he concluded his funeral address (*hesped*) with a few sentences in Hebrew in tribute to the great Hebrew scholar whom we all honoured.

I was standing next to an old friend and admirer of Sokolow's, a world-famous Hebraist renowned for his learning and for his irreverent wit. I think he was a Lithuanian *maskil*. "What did you think of Rabbi Hertz's funeral address on Sokolow?" he was asked. "Actually," he replied, "it would have been better if it had been the other way round – for two reasons. First of all it would have been a better address, and secondly...anyhow."

There are some witticisms that are better left unuttered and maybe unrecorded.

(Published in the *CJRA Newsletter*, Passover/April 1986, pp.24-6.)

Reflections: when two Palestinian soldiers held a spirited Chanucah party for a group of children in Notting Hill

My parents came to England at the turn of the century from Lithuania, then under the Tsar. They were glad to escape. They did not settle – as most of their generation did – in the East End of London, but joined the small Jewish community in Notting Hill. There was a small Federation synagogue, though no officiating rabbi. The newcomers were artisans, petty traders, shopkeepers and tailors; most had young families.

Sometime during the First World War, a number of *baalebatim* [heads of household] who were not particularly keen on the local Talmud Torah began to discuss the possibility of introducing a more modern approach to the education of their children. In particular, they took up the idea of Hebrew as a spoken language. This was stimulated by the then-current interest in Zionism and the publication of the Balfour Declaration in 1917, which said Britain would be in favour of establishing a Jewish national home in Palestine.

There was also the example of the *Ivrit b'Ivrit* [Hebrew taught by the direct method] courses organized in the East End by the Rev J K Goldbloom, and the encouragement of such scholars as Leon Simon. A remarkable coincidence gave these ideas a chance of realization. When the war ended, the community discovered that there were, in Notting Hill, two Palestinian Jews who had served in military units supporting the Allied war effort, and who were unable to return to their homes. They agreed to serve as teachers of spoken Hebrew, and the classes were established in a disused grocery shop in Kensington Park Road, almost opposite the synagogue.

The children, aged between six and twelve, were split into two groups. They included Kopul Rosen, later a rabbi and founder of Carmel College; Abe Herman (Harman), later Israeli ambassador to the United States and President of the Hebrew University; and my older brother John, who became a senior engineer in the *Rutenberg Electric Company* in Haifa. My younger brother, Henry (Zvi), who is today well known for his original work in Israel on solar energy, was not a pupil – he was too young.

Towards the end of 1920, the teachers decided to put on a Chanukah entertainment, to show the parents what their children had achieved. It began with a short dramatic presentation, in Hebrew, of the story of Hannah and her seven sons. According to tradition, Hannah was a Jewish matron in Jerusalem who swore that she and her children would rather give up their lives than offer sacrifices in the Temple in honour of Antiochus, the tyrannical Syrian overlord.

Hannah was played by one of the oldest girls in the group – I believe she was an older sister of Abe Herman – and we, as her 'children', ran around the stage demonstrating that we, too, would follow her example. The play was followed by Hebrew songs. Of these, I remember only one, which recalls the victory of the Maccabeans over Antiochus in 165 BCE:

Yelodim veyeledoys
Madlikim nairoys, nairoys rabim
Lezaicher gvuroys hamakabim
[Repeat]
Antiyochus roshoh mais
Noflo yovon kuloh
Uvetsiyoyn hurom nais
Hurom nais hage'uloh.
[Boys and girls are kindling,
Kindling many lights,
In 'memberance of heroic deeds
By Maccabean knights.
Antiochus the vile is dead,
No longer rules our nation,
While Zion's flag is now raised high,

The flag of liberation.]

On recalling this song, I suddenly realized that we had been learning not *Ivrit* but *Ivris*, with a typical Lithuanian pronunciation and accentuation. The tune, which I still find stirring, was probably taken from a Slavonic marching or drinking song. At some stage, we kindled the lights, and the celebrations concluded with a party of soft drinks and latkes.

In due course, our teachers were able to return to Palestine. One of them became an important figure in the *Egged* Bus Co-operative. The classes dissolved, and the children continued their Jewish education, either through the local Talmud Torah or through private tuition.

Childhood recollections after a very long time-lapse are bound to be blurred and, occasionally, completely imaginary. But some experiences of that Chanucah celebration over seventy-five years ago still retain for me a certain freshness and vividness. It was my first public Chanucah party.

(Published in *The Jewish Chronicle*, 13 December 1996, p.25.)

Sir Nevill Mott, Nobel Laureate, CH

A tribute by David Tabor

Nevill Mott was born in 1905 and died in 1996. He was a distinguished theoretical physicist of international renown and was one of the father-figures of Solid-State physics. After an honours degree in Mathematics in Cambridge, he spent a considerable period in his mid-twenties in the two great European centres of the New Physics – Copenhagen and Gottingen – and returned to Britain inspired by Quantum Mechanics and Wave Mechanics. But he had also acquired first-hand personal acquaintance with the leaders of the New Physics, many of whom were Jewish or partly Jewish. When he was appointed Professor at Bristol in 1933, Hitler was already taking over Germany and very soon European scientists of Jewish lineage were seeking refuge and support. Nevill Mott and many distinguished British scientists did the best they could to help at a time when there was unemployment among British academics and opposition in some circles to the granting of posts to foreign scientists. Nevill never wavered in his humane attitude. He took into his laboratory half-a-dozen German-Jewish refugee scientists. In addition he and his wife acted as sponsors and guarantors of two refugee children from Czechoslovakia and so enabled them to live out their lives in the freedom of England. Throughout his life he showed himself to be a keen supporter of minorities, a vocal critic of apartheid and sympathetic to Jewish causes.

He came to Cambridge in 1955 as Cavendish Professor and became active in University affairs. At that time I was attached to a group led by Philip Bowden who was on the staff of the Physical Chemistry Department, though his research interests were not particularly close to those of that Department. A few years later after many inter-departmental discussion and, I guess, as a result of Nevill's influence,

Bowden resigned from Physical Chemistry and was made a Reader in Physics and his research group became a sub-department of the Cavendish. There was great excitement at our new sub-departmental status and Nevill Mott's name was on all our lips. It even became a household name and was often invoked by our children who would ask – what is new today about Nevill Mott? At that time we were introducing our children to the Hebrew Grace (*Birchat Hamazon*) chanted around the table on Friday evening and Saturday lunch. The liturgy includes a phrase referring to the Lord of Salvation and of Consolation – in Hebrew *Yeshuot ve Ne-cha-mot*. Our younger son found that Nevill Mott was more homely and familiar than *Nechamot* and – perhaps in a playful mood – substituted his name in place of the Hebrew original. As a result for the next year or so, Nevill Mott's name became an integral part of the Sabbath grace. This happened many, many years ago and the children have long since left home. But when Hanna and I recite the Sabbath grace and reach the appropriate phrase, occasionally we recall those times nearly forty years ago when the children were around the table, and Nevill Mott was nobly paired with the Lord of Salvation.

When Nevill resigned from his position of Master of Caius College, I saw him quite often at morning coffee at the Cavendish cafeteria and we often discussed social, political and religious issues. I remember in particular our discussions in the 1970s. In 1973 Israel had been almost cut in two by Syrian tanks (the Yom Kippur War) and in that period in Soviet Russia, Jewish refuseniks and dissidents were being harassed and imprisoned by the Communist regime. On both issues I found Nevill to be very supportive and affirmative, not only privately but also in public. In these and similar discussions I was immensely impressed with the moral strength of his approach and his conviction that ultimately, somehow, right and decency would surely prevail.

On one occasion I asked him why, in view of his opposition to apartheid and his support of the underprivileged, he was pro-Israel and not pro-Arab in the

Middle East dispute. His answer was in five words: "You must make your choice." This was not a snap decision but the result of deep thought as I discovered on another occasion when the issue was raised amongst a group of academics. His pro-Israel attitude was also shown by his active part in advising Israel on its scientific and educational policies.

Nevill was of Huguenot descent but had little interest in religion until he reached his sixties. He then felt the need for more open discussion by scientists about their religious beliefs. He approached scientists whom he knew and asked them to contribute a chapter on their views in a book he was editing entitled *Can Scientists Believe?* He certainly believed; but his comments to me when it was published in 1991 were - why are we so keen on dogma and ritual? His own approach was almost entirely in terms of ethics and morals and contained little support of doctrine.

Nevill remained active in his scientific work until a couple of weeks before his death. He wrote articles, edited books in his chosen field, engaged in lively discussion and also pursued his humanitarian, social and religious interests. It seemed as if he could go on for ever. His motivation is best expressed in the following true episode. Some years ago a distinguished Cambridge Professor died in his early sixties and I attended his memorial service. When I came out I found myself standing next to Nevill and I wondered if any words were necessary or even seemly. Nevill was a man of grand silences – I am not and I felt that I should break the silence in what turned out to be a dialogue with one speaker.

I said: "Sad business." Nevill nodded. Then I said: "It's a great pity he died so young." Nevill nodded. Then finally I added: "I suppose it is simply one of the hazards of being alive." Nevill nodded and I thought our 'dialogue' had ended. Then suddenly his whole expression changed, his face lit up, his eyes sparkled and he said: "But David, it's worth it."

These few words summarize with typical succinctness his attitude to life, to work and all else.

Yehi zichrono li-vracha [May his memory be for a blessing].

(*CJRA Newsletter*, Passover/April 1997, pp.23-4; based on a talk given to the Cambridge Jewish Cultural Association on 9th December 1996.)

Cambridge: 1936-1939

I came to Cambridge in 1936 to complete a PhD project I had begun at Imperial College in London. They were turbulent times with Moseley in the East End, Mussolini in Italy, Hitler in Germany, imminent treason trials in Russia, Civil War in Spain, German bombs in Guernica. Cambridge students were very much involved in the Spanish struggle for democracy against Franco's fascist army, and I recall a passionate public meeting on this issue in the Corn Exchange; indeed, some students, such as John Cornford and G C Maclaurin, volunteered and died in the International Brigade.

For Jewish students the issues were different. We were beginning to sense the danger to German Jewry of Hitler's anti-Semitic campaign, but none of us ever imagined what would emerge after the end of World War II: the *Shoah* was beyond belief – but true. In those pre-war years many of us sought comfort in our involvement in Judaism and in Zionism youth activities, but few of us believed that within the next ten years a Jewish state would be established and internationally recognized. It is ironical to recall that, in this sombre period of history, several madcap Marx Brothers films were released for general distribution. Two or three of these were shown alternating weekly, the whole series lasting, I believe, for two terms. At that time the Arts Cinema did not exist: the films were shown in a building which, out of term, was used as an auction room for furniture. Undergraduates, graduates and residents alike saw these films at least once: their jokes became part of current conversation and we all became hooked 'Marxists'. I still recall sixty years later the fervour of the audience.

The most immediate issue for Cambridge Jewish students themselves was the founding of a body – the Cambridge University Jewish Society (CUJS) – which brought together all segments of student activity. The jewel in the crown was the synagogue in Thompson's Lane. It was beautifully designed, with the small women's gallery (opposite the historic Ark) which had just enough seating to accommodate the women students and some residents (not one visiting Chief Rabbi ever raised the question of a *mechitsa* [barrier separating men and women]). The seats in the main body of the *shul* were individual chairs of wood arranged in rows with flaps at the back to hold the *siddurim* [prayer books] and *chumashim* [Pentateuchs] for the worshippers in the row behind. The dining room could be used for meetings and Friday evening meals though, in fact, no meals were provided during the first six months because Passover in 1938 occurred during term, and the students decided not to contaminate the crockery with *chometz* [leaven]: for that year, Pesach, as far as concerned utensils, was *glatt* ['extra'] kosher.

Those students and residents who had been in Cambridge before 1937 were aware of our 'homelessness' as a Jewish community; for all of us the building in Thompson's Lane was marvellous. It also had, and still retains, some unique attributes. It was funded by alumni and other benefactors. It has no affiliations to any other body. It is held in trust for the Cambridge University Jewish Society, the Trustees being responsible for the fabric but not for the way the synagogue is run. On the whole the system seems to have worked well for the last sixty years.

The foundation stone was laid by Sir Robert Waley-Cohen (President of the United Synagogue) in April 1937 and a short service followed. The cleric officiating read the Hebrew inscription (now in the entrance hall) and in the excitement mispronounced *Cantabrigia* (which was in Hebrew characters) in a most embarrassing way for those of us (including Maurice Plotnick) within earshot. There was no hitch in the dedication of the synagogue itself in October 1937. Those officiating included the Vice Chancellor, the Chief Rabbi (Hertz), a Reform rabbi and distinguished members of the Anglo-Jewish community; but for some reason, the University Reader in Rabbinics did not attend.

Rabbi Hertz gave a very moving address in which he emphasized the role of the synagogue as a place of study, and the whole event was reported enthusiastically in the *Cambridge Evening News*.

The services on Saturdays were attended by all – orthodox, reform and traditional – wearing their gowns and squares as well as their *tallitot* [prayer shawls]. The service began at 10.30am with *Ein Kamocha* and finished before noon, reputedly so that students could attend their twelve o'clock lectures. (Saturday lectures were very common in those hardworking days.) At that time there was a Jewish house at the Perse School (Hillel House) and the pupils and the House Master, Harry Dagut, would walk from their main building, then near the Catholic Church, to Thompson's Lane if the weather permitted. I have a warm recollection of Mr Dagut and in 1937, when *Succot* [Tabernacles] was out of Term, I celebrated the festival with the pupils at Hillel House and was crowned *Hatan Torah* [Hebrew: bridegroom of the Torah – the person who finishes the reading of the Torah as part of the yearly cycle]. Six years later I was a real *hatan* when I married Hanna in Australia during World War Two. Sadly, Harry Dagut died during the war, and after a few years Hillel House was closed.

There were a few Jewish families in Cambridge and they were very hospitable to the Jewish students. They also did what they could to help Jewish refugees from Germany who began to arrive in increasing numbers after 1938. There were also refugee academics who found positions in Cambridge but most of these were assimilated and made little contribution to Jewish life. One striking exception was David Daube, a recognized authority on Roman law and an outstanding example of the Frankfurt orthodoxy. Another whose name we still recall was Hermann Lehmann.

The main senior figures in Jewish student life were Richard (later Lord) Kahn, senior treasurer of CUJS; Charlie Fox who, when asked, gave a charming (frequently repeated) Yom Kippur sermon on whether there are any new ethical systems; Sydney Goldstein (mathematician) who later overhauled the Haifa Technion and converted it, at great cost to his health, into a modern, prestigious institution. The most influential individual was Herbert Loewe, University Reader in Rabbinics, a man of outstanding integrity, most punctilious in his observance but prepared to co-operate academically with Claude Montefiore, the leader of Reform. Together they edited a remarkable collection of Rabbinic teachings entitled *A Rabbinic Anthology,* and the comments introduced by the editors still make fascinating reading...

Undoubtedly my closest friend was Aubrey (Abba) Eban. He was reputed to have obtained the highest marks ever awarded in the Hebrew Tripos. We knew one another from the Young Zionist Movement and he encouraged me to read modern Hebrew literature. We were both active in the Inter-University Jewish Federation (IUJF), as well as in the Cambridge University Jewish Society (CUJS), of which Eban was the first president. Whenever the government published an important paper on the future of Palestine and/or Zionism, public discussion would be held in Cambridge at which Eban would be the star speaker and the defender of Zionist interests. He was already considered as a serious thinker in British Zionism. When in 1987 he was invited to Cambridge to celebrate the fiftieth anniversary of the CUJS, he did not say much about CUJS but gave a brilliant speech about the political problems facing Israel. As I left the meeting I ran into Marcus Bower, and he remarked in his breezy manner that in style and construction, Eban's talk had the same quality as the talks he had heard from him fifty years ago. Not quite true but near enough.

By the end of 1939 I was folding up my affairs in Cambridge. This was a period during which Jewish students came in increasing numbers from London University Colleges, refugees arrived from parts of Europe not yet overrun by Hitler, and there was a flood of Jewish evacuees from urban centres in danger of bombs.

When, after the war, I returned with my wife to England, the whole world seemed to have been turned upside down. In Cambridge itself, Jewish life and Jewish student life had undergone great changes but Thompson's Lane was still very much the centre of our religious and communal activity.

(This is a shortened version of the article originally published in the *CJRA Newsletter*, Passover/April 1998, pp.25-6.)

David Tabor

Funeral eulogies:
1964-95

David Tabor

Memorial address to Charles Fox
Sunday, 8th November 1964

We have come together today to pay tribute to the memory of Charles Fox, our oldest Jewish resident and the senior Jewish member of the University. I had hoped that this appreciation would have been given by Dr Leslie Harris and I am sure he would have liked to have done so: but he has not been well and has asked me to do so in his place. I have made very full use of the many valuable notes that Dr Harris prepared.

Charles Fox was born in London in 1876, one of four children. His father was not blessed with worldly success and the children must have had considerable difficulty in their early education. Nevertheless they achieved considerable academic and professional distinction. His older brother, for example, was Chief Government Scientist, a Fellow of the Royal Society and achieved a Knighthood.

Charles himself attended the old Jewish Free School; he left early to become a pupil-teacher and, much encouraged by his mother, proceeded to educate himself. He taught himself Latin, then French, and would trudge once a week to the Huguenot Church in West London in order to hear the French Language. He won a scholarship to Christ's College and, to equip himself for his further studies, taught himself Greek. At Cambridge as an undergraduate he had a brilliant career and achieved a double first in Natural Sciences. By the turn of the century he was thus well equipped as a scientist, a humanist and a classicist. He had always shown an interest in psychology and in education and studied both these subjects under Oscar Browning, the noted Principal of the Cambridge University Training College for schoolmasters. When Browning retired, Charles Fox succeeded him and played a pioneering part in spreading his ideas on educational psychology amongst future schoolmasters.

This is not the place, and I am not the person, to speak of his professional attainments as an educationalist. We have with us here, indeed we are honoured to have with us here, Professor Lloyd, the present Principal of the Teachers' Training College and I hope that on some future occasion he may tell us something of Charles Fox's contributions to his field of activity, and of the intimate interest he took in the subsequent welfare of his students. I would, however, like to quote from the preface to his book on Educational Psychology. This was written forty years ago and was dedicated – and this is characteristic of Charles Fox – to his mother whose memory he revered. Dealing with the newfangled mental tests he wrote: "Testers have lost their mental balance and are confusing administrative with psychological procedure, so that devices invented for rapidly marking large numbers of answers have been erected into laws of the working of the mind. Hence we are offered tests in which the examinee no longer answers questions but merely selects a stupid answer forced on him by the examiner."

I do not know how much of Charles Fox's educational theories remain valid today but in this paragraph one sees him forty years ahead of his time, clear, direct, unassuming and without humbug, features which characterized him throughout his life.

In the 1920s Charles Fox was one of the Senior Jewish Dons in residence. His contemporaries were Israel Abrahams, Reader in Rabbinics, Israel Hersch, founder of the now defunct Jewish house at the Perse School, Redcliffe Salamon, Leslie Harris [and] Richard Kahn. Apart from the Jewish Dons and Undergraduates there were practically no Jewish residents and Charles Fox would hold Saturday afternoon 'squashes' for Jewish Undergraduates at Warkworth House, which was then the home of the Teachers' Training College. These social occasions must surely still be remembered with gratitude by Jewish students who were in Cambridge forty years ago. At that time he was Senior Treasurer of the

University Jewish Society and their representative on the aristocratic Anglo-Jewish Association. A little later when I came to Cambridge I remember the Saturday sermons he used to give in the Synagogue to the Perse boys from Hillel House. Those of us of my generation regarded him, I think, with the sort of quizzical affection which we have all retained.

In 1940, in conjunction with Harry Dagut, the House Master of Hillel House, he established the Cambridge Jewish Residents' Association and it is fitting that this body should, in fact, be honouring his memory today, together with Jewish Dons, Jewish students and the present Principal of the Teachers' Training College.

I would like to conclude by saying a few words about Charles Fox as a Jew and his ideas on Judaism as they appeared to me. In 1876 when Charles Fox was born there were fewer than 60,000 Jews in the whole of Britain. The United Synagogue with five constituent Synagogues was only six years old. The Federation of Synagogues was not to be founded for another eleven years. The large influx of Jews from Eastern Europe that was to change the size and complexion of Anglo Jewry almost out of recognition was still to come. By the time Charles Fox had acquired his degree at Cambridge University the Eastern European immigration was still only in mid-flood.

Charles Fox grew up at a time of enlightenment, tolerance, progress and liberalism. Those of you who have read Morris Joseph's classical work *Judaism as Life and Creed* published in 1903 (that is when Charles Fox was 27 years of age), will recognize in his approach the emphasis on rationalism characteristic of his day, the sweet reasonableness with which he justifies Jewish belief in God, the absolute confidence with which he faces the inevitability of progress and Messianic Days "around the corner". It is no accident that Charles Fox was, in fact, a member of Morris Joseph's congregation. One might indeed say that Morris Joseph provided the basis of Jewish religious faith in terms of contemporary sentiment; Charles Fox provided the exact counterpart in the area of ethics and morality.

For Charles Fox there was no problem of faith. He was one of those men who are lucky in their basic convictions. His main concern was with ethics and his fascination with the thought that *no* new morality could ever be conceived. This formed a constant theme of his sermons and his Jewish thoughts: for it meant, to him, that in the ancient Jewish ethic all other ethic[s] and all morality were contained. Today perhaps our problems are different. We are probably less concerned with the possibility of new moral concepts than with the basic question as to whether morality requires the sanction of religion at all. To a Jew of Charles Fox's background such an issue presented a problem which he recognized, but it was not a problem which affected him. He stood firm in his faith.

In the 1930s when I first came to Cambridge, those of my generation were profoundly concerned with the cultural, social and political problems of the Jew, and especially the problem of Jewish survival. At that time it seemed to us impossible that a conscientious Jew could be a non-Zionist, that Charles Fox could have been indifferent. His attitude seemed a relic of an earlier era when anti-Semitism was on the wane, when progress was in the ascendant, when the very idea of the physical annihilation of Jewry seemed inconceivable.

And yet you must not think that Charles Fox's Judaism remained for ever linked to the influences of his Victorian youth. When he was well over eighty years of age he visited the Holy Land for the first time. It was no longer Palestine under British rule but the State of Israel. He was very much moved by what he saw and shortly after he paid a second visit. He was greatly impressed with the land reclamation, with the Hebrew University, with the agricultural settlements, with the Kibbutzim, their schools and their pedagogic system. He was still young enough in spirit at the ripe age of eighty-six to change his attitude: he became a keen and enthusiastic pro-Israeli.

Charles Fox was an excellent classical Hebraist. His Jewish library was scholarly and impressive. He took his Judaism seriously. He harmonized within himself the simple faith of his youth, the Judaistic scholarly interests of his enquiring mind, and in his last years, a warm feeling of admiration for the achievements of the Jews of Israel.

In his personal relationships he was sometimes brusque; but below this, at a very small depth below this, lay a warm and charitable personality. He was indeed a hospitable and generous man. Dr Leslie Harris, who knew him longer and better than any other member of our present community, has remarked that when one thinks of Charles Fox the attributes that at once come to one's mind are absolute integrity and uprightness. Of him the Psalmist has truly written: "Who shall ascend the hill of the Lord? Or who shall stand in his holy place? He that hath clean hands and a pure heart, who hath not lifted up his soul unto vanity, nor sworn deceitfully. He shall receive the blessing from the Lord and righteousness from the God of his salvation."

(Printed with minor alterations in the Fiftieth Anniversary issue of the *CJRA Magazine*, Passover/April 1990, pp.10-12.)

Laci ('Latzi') Ladislav Lax 1967

We have gathered here today to pay our last respects to Tzvi ben David ['Latzi'] Lax.

There are some men who are all intellect, some who are all manners and mannerisms, some who are all heart and feeling – Latzi was one of those. In his relation to people, to events, to situations, to friends and relatives, to anybody he met - colleagues at work, nurses in hospital – he was a warm and outgoing personality.

Latzi was a good Jew devoted to his people and its fortunes. He took great pride in Israel and shared in her victories and in her troubles. Only a few days ago he gladly made available his home and his garden for a function in aid of Israel although he was already a sick man away from home in hospital. The cause of Israel was very near his heart.

To those of us who were his friends, we saw in him not only a warm friend but a devoted husband, a fond father who loved his son, a loyal brother and brother-in-law, a favourite uncle, an affectionate son-in-law. To his family we can say nothing. Our rabbis, who understood human nature very well, long ago recognized that on such an occasion no words of condolence or comfort can have any meaning. Their grief is too large for words and nothing but the passage of time can make their loss seem more acceptable, more bearable.

But it is for us who are here amongst the living to express our few words of appreciation and pay tribute to his memory. Latzi was a man of great generosity of spirit. He enjoyed life and made all who had contact with him feel that life was worth living. He was a man who had no bitterness in his heart and who bore his illness with great courage – in his quiet way he was indeed a very brave man. He was a warm man and a good man. He was a man of good name. In the whole vocabulary of virtues there is no higher praise.

We honour his memory. תהי מנוכתו שלום [Hebrew: May he rest in peace].

Mr Henryk Fleischer

A tribute published in *The Cambridge News,*
Tuesday, 16th January 1968

After a long illness, patiently borne, Mr Henryk Fleischer of 76 Hill Road recently passed away at the age of 74. His death removes from the scene a staunch supporter of the British way of life and a keen protagonist of British democracy.

Henryk Fleischer was born in Lemberg (Lvov) in Austrian Poland towards the end of the last century, but spent most of his adult and married life in Krakow. As a result of an accident during childhood he lost his sight, but with the help of his family and learning Braille he overcame this disability to an astonishing degree. With great perseverance he was able to equip his lively and enquiring mind with a vast store of knowledge and understanding of history, economics, politics, comparative religion and philosophy. He also cultivated a discerning love for classical music.

In Krakow, where he was active in the family business, he joined the English Club. From 1930 onwards, together with his wife, he paid a visit every year to England where he regularly attended the Liberal Summer School. In 1939 the war broke out during his visit to this country and he and his wife made their home in Cambridge. The spiritual confidence and strength that sustained him in his own physical affliction supported him too in the face of war, the loss of his family and the ruin of his personal fortunes in Poland. In all these tribulations he was nobly aided by his wife.

In Cambridge, Henryk Fleischer made many friends through the International Club, through the pupils to whom he taught French and German, and through his participation in WEA classes. His strong attachment to life, his cheerful optimism, his independence and good spirits, his broad intellectual interests won the regard and esteem of all those who knew him. Shortly before his death he provided funds that enabled the local Jewish Community to purchase a Scroll of Law that had been rescued from the destruction of Central European Jewry.

With his death a large circle of friends will feel that a courageous and generous spirit has passed away. He will be widely missed.

At the Funeral of Rosie Harris (July 1971)

There are many people here who knew Rosie Harris longer and perhaps better than I did. I am their mouthpiece. I knew Rosie for well over thirty years but I got to know her more closely when I returned to Cambridge at the end of the war with a young wife and a young family. At that time Leslie Harris was the Chairman of the Jewish Residents' Association and I was the Secretary. It was in those years that Leslie Harris set the pattern of community affairs that we have with us today – and it is a sad thought that it was Leslie Harris who took the initiative in acquiring a site for Jewish burials in Cambridge.

In those years, when we most needed it, Rosie was wonderfully hospitable and kind. There are many other residents who experienced her hospitality and kindness. To us, and here I speak for my wife too, she was more like an older sister or a young aunt; she was like a close relative as well as a dear friend. Rosie was a woman of charm, reserve and great nobility of character and there was not the least touch of pretence or affectation in her make-up. She was always at ease with herself and with the world. I always think of the way she walked, upright with a quiet dignity and serenity – and her bearing was a true reflection of her character.

Rosie Harris was lucky in many things: in her marriage which was happy and harmonious to an exemplary degree, in her children whose careers she followed with great, if somewhat withdrawn pride, in her daughters-in-law, whom she regarded with great esteem and affection, in her grandchildren who gave her so much pleasure, and of course in her friends who all so admired and loved and respected her. But those of us who have lived a little know that this luck is not really luck, it is not chance at all; it is the reflection of her own character and personality. Her happy marriage, the fulfilment she found in her children, their wives and families, the affection and esteem of her friends and acquaintances, all these are the response of others to a wonderful person.

Rosie was not lucky in her health but she conquered ill-health and physical discomfort because to complain was completely against her nature. She was a member of a family renowned in the Jewish community for its Jewish scholarship and uprightness. From her family she inherited and cultivated two things: a very good knowledge of the Hebrew language and its literature, and those attributes that go to make up a true gentlewoman.

She leaves behind her husband – her close companion for over forty years – her sons, her daughters-in-law, her grandchildren and a host of sorrowing friends. Her passing is a great and grievous loss to us all.

Of her I may use the old Aramaic saying

חבל על דאבדין ולא נשכחין

Alas for those who have gone for their like we shall not see again – we shall not easily find a lady of Rosie's quality and calibre.

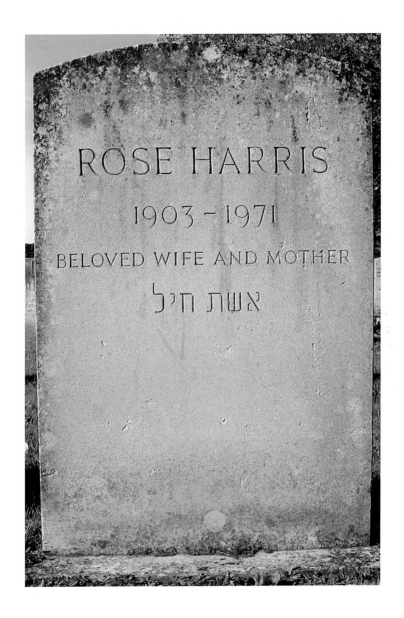

The Funeral of Leslie Harris
(26 June 1973)

Almost exactly two years ago we came together here to pay our last respects to Rosie Harris. Leslie was here, quiet, a little bemused and not perhaps yet aware of the tremendous blow that had befallen him. Today we meet to accompany him to his last resting place. His life with Rosie was such a happy one that it is hard to think of the one without thinking of the other. I recall that beautiful biblical elegy: "They were lovely and pleasant in their lives; and now, in death, they are no longer divided." Their passing within the context of the Cambridge Jewish community marks the end of an epoch.

I knew Leslie for early forty years but it was only after the war that, returning to Cambridge with a young family, I learnt to know him and Rosie better. Their home extended its welcome to all in the Jewish community and many, especially of the older residents, will remember with gratitude the kindness and graciousness of their hospitality. Leslie came from an Anglo-Jewish family that had been settled in this country for over 200 years and he had no trace of that hostility that sometimes exists between Jews from Eastern and Western Europe – he had no trace of that bitterness between orthodox and non-orthodox which now disfigures the face of Anglo-Jewry.

Leslie's father was an orthodox rabbi who, in the early days of this century, showed remarkable independence and strength of character. He was a Zionist when the official line of the Anglo-Jewish Ministry was non- or anti-; and in World War I he was a pacifist at a time when patriotism was at its most hysterical level. Leslie inherited and adopted both of these viewpoints. He was, indeed, a natural pacifist for by temperament he was a gentle and sweet man whose kindness overflowed in his contacts with almost everybody with whom he made contact. One might say of him that he loved peace and pursued it. He was also a lifelong Zionist – not perhaps politically or organizationally, for he was not that sort of man, but intellectually and culturally – and he took a deep and abiding interest in Judaism and especially in Hebrew.

It is right that on this occasion I should recall that Leslie Harris was Chairman of the Jewish Residents' Association at the end of the war. It was under his Chairmanship that we negotiated with the Borough Council for the purchase of a plot of land for Jewish burial. It was under his Chairmanship that many of the features of our present communal affairs were first established. Our debt to him is a very real one.

Leslie was a man of many parts. He was a distinguished scientist who played a pioneering role with Nobel Prizewinner Sir Frederick Gowland Hopkins in the early days of vitamin research. One of his little books on vitamins is still a most readable and enlightening work in this field – but I am not the person and this is not the time or place to talk of these things. He was also a fine amateur artist with paint and pencil. He was a very gifted sculptor, far beyond the level of amateur performers. He had a very good ear for music and a very good feeling for linguistics and phonetics. He was an enthusiastic student of languages, which in his last years he directed more and more to Hebrew.

But above all it is Leslie the man whom we recall today; a man blessed with a marriage which was marvellously harmonious; with children whose careers he followed with great pride; with daughters-in-law who regarded him with great affection; with grandchildren who gave him endless pleasure; and with numerous friends, colleagues and acquaintances who appreciated Leslie for what he was – a quiet, gentle, peaceful man, in some ways a simple, I might almost say an innocent man in its best sense, a man of integrity, a lovable man.

יהי זכרונו לברכה May his memory be for a blessing.

The Funeral of Erusha Solomon (notes)

(24 May 1904 – 4 August 1973)

B orn in 1904 in Karachi – father Abraham Reuben – President of Bene Israel.....her brother Simon also.

Grew up attached to her community and used to idea of communal service.

Married Dr Solomon, came to England with daughter Sophia – 1950.

Great help to her husband in work as a medical practitioner.

After his death she was active with other Jewish ladies in Cambridge, active in the British Legion, Women's Section, City Branch, especially helping fund-raising for convalescent homes for ex-servicemen and families.

We think of her loyalty to her community, in Pakistan and in England, her loyalty to her religious tradition, her loyalty to her husband and his profession, her loyalty to her friends and, especially here today, her loyalty and love to her relatives, and especially her daughter.

The funeral of Jack Kenden
30th October 1973

We have come together here to pay our last respects to Jack Kenden. It seems only a few months ago that we visited his home when he was in mourning for his mother, and it is a sad thought that his own passing away should come so soon after.

Jack Kenden was a warm-hearted, outward going man. He was a member of a very large family, all of whom regarded him with great esteem and affection – he was greatly appreciated by his in-laws and it is a measure of their love for him that they have rallied so generously to support Josi in her time of grief. His close friends in Cambridge have also shown how much they have felt for him and his family – I would mention the Lasks and especially the Bogens for the way they have rallied.

But it is chiefly as a warm-hearted family man that we recall him today. His greatest pleasure and satisfaction was in his wife and children. To his son who has recently passed his Bar Mitzvah, to his daughter and above all to his widow we express our sincerest condolences. Their loss is irreplaceable and no words can change this.

But it is right and proper to pay our respects in this way to a good husband, a good father, a good family man, a good friend indeed and a good man.

יהי זכרונו לברכה May his memory be for a blessing.

Funeral of Manny Porter
מלך בן ירוחם
10ᵗʰ May 1974

W e have come here today to pay our last respects to Manny Porter, and it would not be right if I did not say a few words on behalf of the Jewish community.

Manny came to Cambridge via Royston nearly fifteen years ago and soon he and his family entered fully and enthusiastically into the life of the small community here. With great energy and in his breezy way he blew the cobwebs out of our provincial approach to many communal matters. For the last decade, together with Max Ratner, he virtually ran or became involved in every aspect of Jewish communal life. He looked after the fabric of the synagogue. I do not know how many times he tried to activate the central heating facilities, he organized the synagogue for the High Festivals, he looked after our finances, and after Max Ratner's departure from Cambridge he became the Chairman of the Residents' Association. To all this he brought his cheerful determination to do whatever was necessary.

During the last few years he was responsible for looking after Jewish burials in Cambridge. He maintained friendly relations with the cemetery authorities and provided all the facilities needed. It is a sad thought that only a couple of weeks ago he invited me to conduct a funeral service for an elderly refugee and when I arrived, there he was with his pile of books quietly but effectively making sure that everything was in order. At the end of the ceremony he stayed behind and discussed with me the possibility of installing a handbasin at the entrance of the cemetery for the use of Jewish visitors. And here today the whole issue is turned on its head.

The wonderful quality about Manny was the willingness he brought to his tasks. There are some people who make things possible – others who make them impossible: some who will always be ready to do things – others who always have excuses for not doing them. Manny was in the first category. He was a willing and devoted servant of the community and he brought to his tasks a cheerful personality, a sense of humour and a ready wit. In these days when so many people rely on others to carry out the various tasks that a community must do it was wonderful to have in Manny such a devoted and unselfish helper. There is in our liturgy a phrase for these people.

העוסקים בצרכי הציבור באמונה Those who participate faithfully in the needs of the community and they are singled out for special praise.

But I cannot refer only to the loss to the community. His loss to his wife and children is irreplaceable and we extend to them our sincerest condolences. There are no words for this.

And then, too, to Turi Goldstein it must be a tremendous blow to lose his manager with whom he worked so harmoniously and so effectively for the last ten years – a loss which he will find terribly hard to replace.

And finally to all his friends and acquaintances the loss of such a man is something we shall feel for many, many years to come.

יהי זכרונו לברכה May his memory be for a Blessing – may he rest in peace.

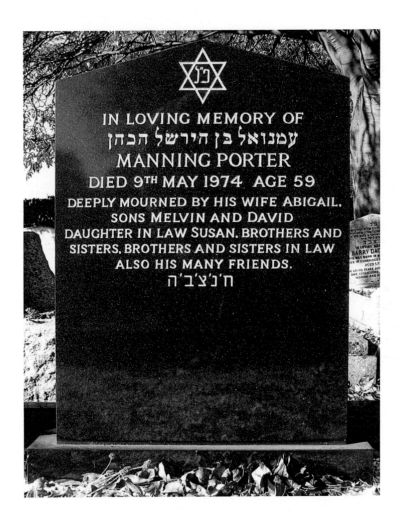

IN LOVING MEMORY OF
עמנואל בן הירשל הכהן
MANNING PORTER
DIED 9TH MAY 1974 AGE 59
DEEPLY MOURNED BY HIS WIFE ABIGAIL.
SONS MELVIN AND DAVID
DAUGHTER IN LAW SUSAN. BROTHERS AND
SISTERS. BROTHERS AND SISTERS IN LAW
ALSO HIS MANY FRIENDS.
ח'נ'צ'ב'ה

Funeral of Paula Goldwater 14th March 1977

We have come here today to pay our last respects to Mrs Goldwater. Nothing that I can say can reduce the sense of loss of her children and grandchildren – but I feel I ought to say a few words on behalf of the Jewish community in Cambridge.

I first met the Goldwaters over forty years ago when I was a young student in Cambridge. My mother, when she would come to see me would sometimes visit them in their little shop in Fitzroy Street, to talk of affairs in general and Jewish affairs in particular. The shop had a warm and friendly atmosphere like the Goldwaters' home itself.

In those years there were very few settled Jewish families in Cambridge and the Goldwaters were amongst the stable element of the community. When the first refugees from Hitler Europe began to arrive in Cambridge, they played their own part in helping the community to cope with the new problems that arose and kept open house as far as was possible. During the war when a large contingent of Jews from London came to settle in Cambridge and when there was a continuous stream of American servicemen, they again pulled their weight. They again showed outstanding hospitality and until quite recently they had American visitors from the war years who would come to see them. After the war the Jews from London began to leave Cambridge and we had to face the difficulties of a shrinking Jewish community. I still recall the discussions we had – I think I was Secretary or Chairman of the Residents' Association in those days – in the Goldwaters' house or in the Jeffreys' house or in the Sunderlands' - discussing ways and means of strengthening Jewish life in Cambridge. In all this activity the Goldwaters remained staunch supporters of the community – with a warm, uncomplicated commitment to their Jewish identity.

They were not very lucky in their health but they were lucky in their children, for they had the joy of seeing both their children married within the fold. After Mrs Goldwater was widowed she found particular pleasure and *nachas* in being able to live close to her married daughter and her grandchildren.

During the last few months she was particularly lucky and happy to be provided with a home within the home of her daughter. A privilege that is denied to many elderly widows and widowers. It is a great tribute to her daughter [Marlene] and to Austin that they took her in so warmly, though I think this must make their loss more acute and more difficult to bear.

Mrs Goldwater was a warm and cheerful woman who was a good friend to many members of the community. She was devoted to her children and grandchildren.

In extending our condolences to her family we recall that her death marks the severing of yet one more link with that small band of Jews who, between the two wars, helped to sustain the Jewish community in Cambridge.

יהי זכרונה לברכה May her memory be for a blessing.

Funeral of Dr Jacob Teicher
19th November 1981

We have come here today to pay our last respects to Jack Teicher and to pay tribute to his life and work.

His life was an epitome of the twentieth century European Jew. He was born in 1904 in the small Galician town of Rudki near Lvov. His father was President of the local Jewish community and had hopes that his son would become a rabbi. The family was uprooted by the First World War and returned to the newly founded Polish State in 1920. But the *numerus clausus* in Poland would have excluded the children from a University education and in 1922 the whole family migrated to Florence. There was a thriving Jewish community there and Jack Teicher studied at the Rabbinical College under Professor Cassuto, one of the outstanding Biblical scholars of our times. He consolidated there the foundations of that tremendous scholarship and learning that informed the whole of his approach to Jewish and cognate studies. He stopped short of being ordained as a rabbi.

At the same time he pursued his secular studies at the University of Florence and took his PhD on a topic dealing with Philosophy in the Middle Ages. Indeed, medieval philosophic studies remained one of his chief intellectual interests throughout his life.

During the second half of the 1930s, Mussolini, under Hitler's influence began the introduction of anti-Jewish legislation and it was partly as a result of this and of his scholarly interests that he was induced to leave Italy. Irwin Rosenthal, himself a refugee from Hitler's Germany, had been in correspondence with Jack Teicher and had suggested that they might collaborate in their research on the writings of Averroes. Jack came to England in 1938 for this purpose. At the same time one of his brothers went to Switzerland where he still lives; the rest of the family returned to Poland. They lost their lives in the Holocaust except for one of Jack's brothers, who fought in the Polish resistance and received the highest awards from the post-war Polish Government.

In 1939 Jack moved to Oxford where he served as private secretary to Dr Schwarzbed, one of the two Jewish members of the Polish Government in exile. One of his tasks was to decipher messages from wartime Poland and translate them into English for transmission to the British and American governments. In this work he was greatly aided by Kate [his wife]. Thus he remained fully informed of what was going on in Poland, what was being perpetrated by the Germans and what was happening to his family and the rest of Polish Jewry.

In 1946 the University of Cambridge appointed Jack Teicher as Lecturer in Rabbinics to fill the gap that had followed the death in 1940 of Herbert Loewe, the former Reader in Rabbinics. This marked the beginning of Jack's connection with the University and with the Jewish community of Cambridge.

Those of us who were in Cambridge at the time recall the intellectual stimulus he brought to both the students and the residents, and the commitment he showed in many important ways - in the invigilation of Jewish students who wished to be excused from taking examinations on the Sabbath or festivals – in the conducting of Jewish burials at a period when the Jewish community had for the first time acquired a separate plot of ground here in the municipal cemetery – in the weekly conversational Hebrew classes that he held for students on Saturday afternoons. I still recall those occasions when on a Sabbath morning service we would suddenly find ourselves short of someone who had promised to read a portion from the *Torah*. Without any notice he would take over and give a faultless reading even of the most difficult passages.

In 1948 he became the first editor of *The Journal of Jewish Studies* and held that post until 1955. In those early years after the war there was a freshness and liveliness in the articles published and a general impression of optimism in this manifest revival of Jewish learning in Europe. He continued to contribute to the general field of Medieval Jewish philosophy, and out of this grew a professional interest in early editions of Hebrew works not previously known to have existed which he unearthed and identified. I understand that he established a firm reputation in this field of Hebrew *incunabula*. He also became involved in various rival theories concerning the Dead Sea Scrolls and I note, with some sadness, that he agreed to speak in January 1982 to Cambridge Jewish Residents on this very subject – a promise that can never be fulfilled.

Jack Teicher was a brilliant linguist: classical languages, Teutonic languages, Romance languages, Slavonic languages and of course Hebrew, Aramaic and Arabic. He had a natural flair for languages. I remember once asking him to recommend a readable Aramaic grammar. He replied that the best method would be to ignore the grammar books and simply read the Aramaic translation of the Bible side-by-side with the Hebrew original. In this way, he assured me, I would acquire a perfect knowledge of the idiom and structure of biblical Aramaic – I suspect he learnt languages himself that way.

He was also a man of immense learning and erudition – not only in Judaica – but in a host of other fields. This made him a lively and well-informed conversationalist: in discussion there could never be a dull moment. He brought to small talk and to scholarship enthusiasm, liveliness, originality, unconventional ideas, critical questioning. His approach was a mixture of Talmudic acumen, Hassidic fervour, perhaps a touch of Italian brio, all coupled with tremendous reserves of knowledge.

Jack was a Fellow of Wolfson College and a long-standing member of the Faculty of Oriental Studies. His scholarship is recognized by the presence here of representatives of his College and his Faculty.

But for most of us, it is Jack Teicher the man and the friend whom we mourn here today. He was not blessed with good health but he was lucky in his marriage for he had a devoted wife and a charming daughter, to whom we express our sympathy on this sad occasion.

May his memory be for a blessing. יהי זכרונו לברכה

ומותר עכשיו להוסיף מילים אחדים בעברית? שפה זו שהיתה
כל כך חביבה עליו.יעקב אריה בן יוסף יצחק טייכר. היה אחד
משרידי הישוב היהודי-הפולני. רכש לו בימי נעוריו ידיעה
עמוקה ביהדות הקלאסית. שתה ממעיינות הפלוסופיה של ימי
הביניים. שלט בחכמת היהדות בת-זמננו, והצתיין במרחב
למודיו ובשנות מחקריו. אנו מאבלים היום על פטירתו – חבל
על דאבדין ולא נשתשכחן.

[Hebrew: May I be permitted to add a few words in Hebrew? The language which was so dear to Jacob Teicher.
He was one of the remnants of the Jewish inhabitants of Poland. In his youth he acquired a deep knowledge of classical Judaism; he drank at the wells of the philosophy of the Middle Ages; he mastered contemporary Jewish wisdom. He excelled in the breadth of his studies and in the years of his research. We mourn today his passing. We sorrow at the loss of one who will not be replaced.]

Funeral of Alexander Bobrow
29th April 1983

We have come here today to pay our last respects to Alexander Bobrow. The years of our life are three score and ten, and sometimes we reach the age of *g'vurot* – the eighties. But to live out a full and active and cheerful life in possession of one's mental faculties until one is almost ninety – he would have been ninety this week – is given to very few of us.

Alexander Bobrow was born in Puisk in the Pale of Settlement in 1893. He was nurtured on the Bible, he greatly relished the dialectics of the Talmud, [and] he was a keen Yiddishist, influenced to some extent by the Russian and Jewish Socialism of his day. In his adolescence he undertook a difficult and successful conquest of the Russian language, which involved not only a linguistic triumph but a transition into a new cultural world. He received a Russian University education and qualified as an analytical chemist in 1915 and worked outside the Pale in his profession.

When he returned to Puisk, which was indeed a frontier town, it was occupied by the Germans and completely cut off from the world. There was famine, starvation and a typhoid epidemic. More and more children became homeless and it was at this stage that he took the initiative with a few friends to open up an orphanage in a disused Talmud Torah where children could be looked after, sheltered and given whatever food could be found. By the time the war ended they had three orphanages with nearly five hundred children, but the burden and responsibility were tremendous, so that only dedicated and spiritually strong leaders could keep them operational. Alexander Bobrow thought of this as perhaps the most challenging and positive contribution that he made to the welfare of his fellow Jews.

When the war ended the American Joint Distribution Committee sent vast quantities of food, medical supplies and clothing. The children were now all looked after but their prospects were far from encouraging. In the early twenties attempts were made to provide them with homes and futures in other countries. A few went to Palestine, some to England and in 1921 a representative from South Africa came and offered a whole group of children a home in Cape Town. The Puisk Committee agreed to do this but only if Alexander Bobrow went with them. That is how he came to South Africa with 160 children and saw them settled.

He married in 1928 and his first and only daughter was born in 1929. After several years as a wandering teacher, he and his wife set up a Jewish Boarding School in Cape Town where they were Principal and Matron for over a dozen years.

In Cambridge we knew him when he came in 1966/7 to prepare his grandson Adam for his Bar Mitzvah and I don't think we shall easily forget the fervour and vigour of his Bar Mitzvah address. He must also have charmed the Clerk of the Weather for the lunch reception in the Gardens of Peterhouse was held under idyllic conditions. After his wife's death (1968) he came to live with his daughter and son-in-law and we saw him regularly at synagogue functions. He was particularly conspicuous at *Simchas Torah* [Rejoicing of the Law] celebrations where, into his early eighties, he out-danced and out-sang the students with enthusiasm and indestructible energy.

Although by background he was a *misnaggid* [Hebrew: 'opponent' of Hassidic Judaism], and what in older days one would call a *maskil* [Hebrew: 'enlightened man'; a follower of the Jewish Enlightenment in the late 18th and 19th centuries], he was by temperament a *chosid* [Yiddish: a follower of Hassidic Judaism], full of optimism, good cheer and high spirits. Whenever he was involved with people he was, I think he would like to hear me say it, [in Russian] – ом был душой общества - he was the life and soul of the party.

After his blindness, which he bore with extraordinary stoicism, he moved to the Dolly Ross Home in 1975 where again he became a leading figure in the social, cultural and Jewish life of the home. He came back to Cambridge for his second grandson's Bar Mitzvah in 1976 and at the age of 83 recited by heart the *Haftorah* – Of him it may be said, as of Moses, **לא נס לחו** [Hebrew: His natural force was not abated].

In his love for Yiddish, for Hebrew, for Jewish culture he exerted an influence which left its mark not only on his family and his grandchildren but on a host of friends and acquaintances.

May his memory be for a blessing.

ועכשיו מותר להוסיף מילים אחדים בעברית? שפה זו שהיתה כל כך חביבה עליו. אלכסנדר אריה לב נולד בזרח אירופה. היה בן של דור נפלה, דור נעלם ונפסק ועוד לא יחזור. הוא ינק מימי ילדותו אהבה עמוקה לספרות התנך, לחכמת התלמוד, לשפה עיידיש, ובימי נעוריו רכש לוידיעה עמוקה בשפה הרוסית ותרבותיו. היה יהודי אופטימיסטי, חגיגי, חיובי, שמח-לב. התלהבותו היתה כזוהר ונגה שהשפיעו לטובה על כל מכיריו. מלא-שנים הלך לעולמו ועליו ועל דורו מותר להביא את המימרה הארמית-

חבל על דאבדין ולא נשתשכחן- יהי זכרונו לברכה.

[Hebrew: May I be permitted to add a few words in Hebrew? The language which was so dear to Alexander Bobrow. He was born in Eastern Europe to a wonderful generation which was even then coming to its end. It will not come again. From his infancy he imbibed a deep love of the literature of the Hebrew Bible, the wisdom of the Talmud, and for the Yiddish language. In his youth he also gained a deep knowledge of Russian language and culture. He was a Jew who was optimistic, cheerful, positive and happy. His enthusiasm shone like a bright star and was a good influence on all his friends. In the fullness of years he has gone to his eternal rest, and for he and his generation we can quote the Aramaic saying:

We sorrow at the loss of one who will not be replaced.
May his memory be for a blessing.]

★★★★★

David added the following note afterwards:

This was written a couple of hours before the funeral on the morning of 29th April. On the previous evening Aaron [Klug] had brought the relevant material and told me a few facts which form the basis of the above.

However, at the time of writing I had not had a chance to read some of his Yiddish poems especially a couple of translations from Bialik – a great favourite of his. These translations are faithful to the original but also have the individual quality of the translator. I wish I had had time to include some reference to his poetic interests in my *hesped*.

Arthur (Turi) Goldstein Hesped 9th February 1984

The Goldsteins are amongst our oldest and closest friends in Cambridge and it is with a special sense of loss that we are here together with you all to pay our last respects to Turi. He would have been 82 in March.

Turi was born in a small township in the old Austro-Hungarian Empire, now in Czechoslovakia. He grew up in farmland and remained attached to the countryside all his life. He trained as an engineer and with the spread of Hitlerism came to England in 1938. His wife was to follow him but before she was able to do so she was swept away and lost in the Nazi Holocaust.

In Cambridge, Turi set about establishing a small factory, using his ingenuity and skills to create products that were timely and effective. At the end of World War II he married Halina Lapin, herself a survivor of the Nazi concentration camps. Together they built up the *Warmex Company* in Cambridge which flourished so successfully that they expanded and moved out to Swavesey years ago. Turi created employment for numerous Cambridge men and women and his achievements were much appreciated by the municipal authorities. He was a model employer and extremely good to his workforce. I recall that we once had a plumber to do some repairs in our house and it turned out that he had been employed at *Warmex*. He didn't know that we were Jews and on one occasion he said, "You know what they say about these people, but as far as I am concerned he was the best boss I ever had." I think most of his employees felt the same way.

Turi was a very gifted and inventive man. He was full of original and practical ideas. But he was also basically a modest man and his demands on life were modest. He was kind and exceptionally generous not only in money matters but also in his human attitude. It overflowed in his work, in his friends, in his support for Jewish and Israeli causes. I would like to think that none of us ever exploited his generosity.

Turi was a man of strong loyalties: to his work, to his family [and] to his Jewish origins. He was strongly attached to traditional Judaism: he once said to me that he found it a good religion. He was much moved by the synagogue services and happy if he could play any part in them. He loved cantorial music (*chazanut*). He observed *Jahrzeits* not only for his family but for the township in which he was brought up and which was made completely *Judenrein* [German: free of Jews] by the Nazis. He was one of the key members of the local Jewish Burial Society, the *Chevra Kaddisha,* and he played an active part in enabling the community to acquire the new plot of burial sites. Maybe it is fitting that he will be the first to be interred in the new plot.

Turi was a generous donor to Jewish charities and was particularly generous in his contributions to Israeli Institutions – the Jewish National Fund, two universities and several hospitals. But he sought no publicity – he gave and for him that was the main thing.

Last but not least he enjoyed his family and treated them with love and consideration.

With Turi's death Cambridge has lost a worthy citizen, the Jewish community has lost a loyal son, Israel has lost a staunch supporter, those who knew him well have lost a dear friend, and his family, to whom we express our deepest condolences, have lost a loving husband, father and grandfather.

יהי זכרונו לברכה May his memory be for a blessing

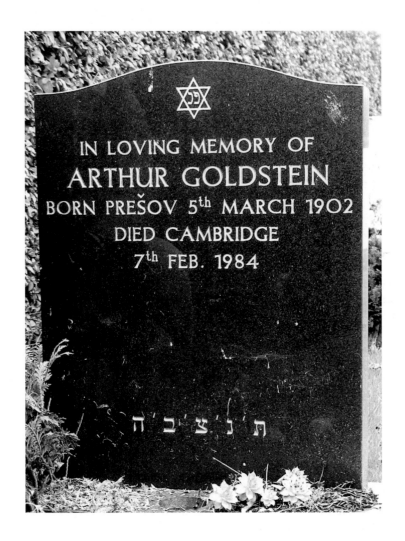

Funeral for Richard Ferdinand Kahn
Monday 12th June 1989

(9th Sivan 5749)

We have come together today to pay our last respects to Richard Ferdinand Kahn, Lord Kahn of Hampstead, or more simply in the Jewish tradition רפאל מנשה בן נפתלי הכהן – R'fael ben Naftali.

This is not the time or the place – and I am not the person – to pay tribute to his academic distinction and his achievement of public honours. I would, however, like to say a few words about Richard Kahn - whom fifty years ago we sometimes call Dick, and even amongst ourselves Dickie - as a Jew, as a member of the Jewish academic fraternity.

Richard was born in August 1905 into a comfortable cultured family in Hampstead. His father, Augustus Kahn (1868–1944), was an undergraduate at St John's College and completed his Mathematical Tripos in 1889. Mathematics seems to have run in the family. His professional career was in Education: but he was also an extremely orthodox and observant Jew. He was an adherent of that form of Judaism associated with a very distinguished German Jewish thinker, Rabbi Samson Raphael Hirsch who, in the middle of the nineteenth century, coined the phrase *Torah im derech eretz*, that is, strict observance of the laws of the Torah, combined with an openness to secular learning. It is not surprising that father Augustus became and remained for many years an active member of the Council of the United Synagogue – the largest synagogal body in this country. Thus Richard was brought up in a household which had a commitment to communal service and combined punctilious and decorous orthodoxy with a thirst for education and culture.

Richard came to Cambridge as an undergraduate in 1924 and took part in local synagogal activities. At that time there was no permanent building and services were held in temporary accommodation. There were only half a dozen Jewish families in Cambridge and probably the only close connections he had were with the Readers in Rabbinics – at first Israel Abrahams and later Herbert Loewe. I know that when I came to Cambridge in 1936 he would visit the Loewes at their home from time to time. He took part in the students' services and on those occasions when it is customary for Jews of priestly descent – that is to say those whose family name is derived from Cohen – to recite the Priestly Benediction, he would do so with devotion and decorum. Of course, when important festivals fell outside term and there were not enough Jews to constitute a religious quorum (ten males) he would go back to his family in London.

His orthodoxy amongst Jewish students and amongst his contemporaries at King's was a byword. He strictly observed the Sabbath and even as a Bursar he would not sign cheques on that day. He was most punctilious in his observance of the dietary laws. He was also prepared to help observant Jewish students and after he acquired senior status as a Fellow at King's – incidentally he may well have been the first practising Jew to be elected to a Fellowship at King's – he readily acted as an invigilator for those students who did not wish to take examinations on the Sabbath.

Richard was in some ways a very private man and none of us knew him very well. However, in local Jewish affairs he accepted the post of Senior Treasurer of the University Jewish Society and held that position until about 1946 when I took over from him. He was also much engaged in the negotiations that led to the planning and establishment of a permanent synagogue in Thompson's Lane. This building was consecrated in 1937 in the presence of the Vice Chancellor and the Chief Rabbi of the time (Rabbi J H Hertz) and Richard remained a valued Trustee of the synagogue for over 40 years (1936 to 1977). It is still in essence the synagogue of the students. At this point I see a group of observant Jewish students who have come to this service. They are young enough to have been his grandchildren. In terms of the fulfilment they find in the synagogue, one might well refer to them as his spiritual grandchildren.

During the period before and during the war he cooperated with Herbert Loewe in helping Jewish refugees from Hitler's Germany – especially academics. When a Jewish Residents' Association was formed he became a member and remained a member for the rest of his life.

World War II was a watershed in the life of many of Richard's generation. As far as Richard was concerned his involvement in Jewish religious activity from that time on faded and I remember seeing him only on rare occasions at synagogue services after 1946. He did not pretend that he was something else. He retained his identity as a Jew with pride and took a positive – if sometimes somewhat critical – attitude to Israel. But observance, ritual and the religious tradition no longer touched him.

Nevertheless, those of us with longer memories will recall with gratitude the contributions he made to Jewish student life in his early years and the long-term contribution he made in connection with the establishment of the synagogue, which remains one of the pivotal points of Jewish student activities in Cambridge.

In his last years there was some turning back and in his quiet retiring way he asked if he could be buried in the Jewish portion of the Cambridge cemetery. That is why we are here today to conduct a traditional Jewish funeral service. He will be interred with his prayer shawl and his phylacteries, which meant so much to him in his youth.

It would perhaps be fitting to end with phrases from the Priestly Benediction:

May the Lord be gracious unto him and give him peace.
Yehi Zichrono li Vrachah
May his memory be for a blessing.

(I am indebted to Raphael Loewe for some early details which were unknown to me. In particular he mentioned that the deceased pronounced his name R'fuel rather than R'fael. This may give some hint as to the provenance of his forebears.)

Irwin Rosenthal
Delivered at the Funeral Service
7th June 1991

Today we come together to pay our last respects to Irwin Rosenthal.

The Rosenthals are amongst our oldest friends in Cambridge. We remember when they first came here over forty years ago and the visits that we paid to one another over that very long period.

Their arrival here was a very great acquisition for Cambridge Jewry, not only because of Irwin's strong commitment to Judaism and Jewish affairs but also because of the warm hospitality they bestowed on Jewish students in Cambridge almost from the first day that they moved into Chesterton Road. On Saturday afternoons one could always meet Jewish undergraduate enjoying their tea and their company.

This is not the occasion to refer to Irwin's sterling educational work for Jews interned during World War II, nor can I say anything about his scholarship. I am not competent to do so – but I greatly treasure a volume of his *Studia Semitica on Jewish Themes* which he inscribed to me nearly twenty years ago. These essays and many of the articles he wrote for learned journals, and for more popular publications, reflect his deep devotion to that type of Judaism which emerged from the *Wissenschaft des Judentums*. It was a combination of traditional Judaism and enlightenment – a strong attachment to Jewish values and practices combined harmoniously with a scholarly and aesthetic appreciation of western culture. Part of this cultural tradition was shown by the deep love he had, and shared with Elizabeth, for classical music and for good books, and a palate for fine wines, tastes that they shared with their children – while his attachment to Judaism was shown by his love of Jewish observance and by his loyal and dedicated membership of the synagogue in Thompson's Lane which, until recently, he attended regularly.

Irwin was a genial man, good company and always neat and spick and span. He was greatly respected by his College at Pembroke as is shown by the fact that a painted portrait of him, commissioned by the College, hangs in one of its public rooms. He enjoyed the contacts that he formed there and the social life that it provided. He also enjoyed walking and for many years would go for walks with Bernard Zeitlyn. He was, indeed, a rounded man at ease in the countryside, at musical concerts, at scholarly conferences, at synagogue services and in the general company of people.

Hanna and I recall with particular pleasure the many occasions on which Irwin and Elizabeth came to us to celebrate the Passover Seder: Irwin always did his bit with considerable "cheyn".

Today we come together to mourn his death, the end of 58 years of happy marriage with Elizabeth, the loss of a loving father and grandfather, the loss of a dear friend.

Yehi Zichrono l'ivracha
May his memory be for a blessing.

Heskell Isaacs
Thursday, 3rd November 1994

We have come here to pay our last respects to our friend Heskell Isaacs who passed away in his 81st year after a short but painful illness, bravely endured.

Heskell's life reads to an outsider like a story from the Arabian Nights, and I am indebted to Jill Young for some of the details and indeed some of the phrases.

He was born and educated in Iraq of a good Jewish family with a rich background in Hebrew and Judaica. He was proficient in Hebrew, French and English and in Arabic language and culture. In his mid-twenties he qualified as a doctor at a French language hospital in Baghdad and served as a Medical Officer in the Iraqi Cavalry. But think of the changes in his life up to then! When he was born in 1913 Iraq was part of the Ottoman Empire. After World War I when Germany and her allies were defeated it became British Mandated Territory – like Palestine. In 1935 it was granted independence as a monarchy and established its own constitution – an amazing mixture of Western ideas and tribal traditions. When World War II broke out pro-Nazi sympathisers tried to take over the country. By the end of the war, in an atmosphere of increasing nationalism and anti-Jewish sentiment. Heskell was somehow able to leave Iraq and reach England. He was in his early 30s.

Two great events took place in the next four years. He met and married Ruth, who became the backbone of the family. Secondly, he re-qualified as a doctor so that he could enter the National Health Service. For the next thirty-five years he ran his own medical practice and some of you may have heard his daughter Ann's account of the full and committed life he led in ministering to his patients and in helping in the training of other General Practitioners. In his forties, in the prime of his life he found time – there is a certain period in life when everything seems possible – to resume his study of Arabic at Manchester University and ultimately to obtain a PhD for research in the History of Medicine, as reflected in medieval Arabic sources. And in this period of full involvement he and Ruth raised a family in the traditions of their people.

After retirement, when he was nearly seventy years old, he came to Cambridge to face a tremendous challenge offered him by Stefan Reif in the Geniza Department of the University Library – to catalogue those Arabic and Judaeo-Arabic medical manuscripts which had not been studied before. It needed a scholar with a knowledge of Hebrew, Arabic and Judaeo-Arabic, a first-hand understanding of medicine and an interest in medical history. He was uniquely qualified for the task.

Those of us who attended his 80th birthday celebration organized by Ruth and the family will recall the tremendous recognition this work gained from scholars in the field. It was a source of great happiness to him, his family and his friends that he lived to see this work in its published form, beautifully produced by the Cambridge University Press (CUP). At that same celebration Mancunians expressed their respect for his linguistic and medical activities in Manchester. For a boy born in Baghdad in 1913 to (becoming) a jubilant research scholar in Cambridge, marks a life of great change and achievement.

But within this saga of extraordinary variety and change lies Heskell the man, overcoming the problems of an immigrant in a new country, serving as a doctor in a new environment, showing good sense and balance in his judgements, liberal in his sentiments, loyal to his Jewish roots, passing on the heritage of his people to his children and grandchildren. When we saw him in hospital surrounded by his wife and family we could see in their lively grandchildren new vigorous branches of that Tree of Life which has sustained the Jewish people throughout their history.

In the dozen years that he and Ruth spent in Cambridge they became active in the Jewish community. Heskell gladly made available to those who sought it, his knowledge of Jewish sources and traditions. He also found time to counsel Jewish prisoners in the local jail. He remained strongly attracted to Judaism but was tolerant and at ease with various trends within the community. However, it was his research which dominated his life during these years in Cambridge. There is a proverb which says that "Old Age is no Joy". But for Heskell, these last ten years were years of tremendous fulfilment, and apart from his last illness, gave him great satisfaction and happiness. In the preface to his book he wrote:

'The presentation of this volume was undertaken in the evening of my life and the work has proved to be more challenging but less tiring than my previous professional career in medicine.'

Here is the balanced judgement of a wise and dedicated scholar, who expresses in typical understatement the stimulus of the challenge, and the joy of his last decade. That is how I shall remember him.

To his dear wife Ruth, his children and his grandchildren we offer our deep sympathy and condolences in their sad loss.

יהי זכרונו לברכה May his memory be for a blessing.

(After I came home from the burial ceremony I thought – In his professional life the practice of medicine was his love – research into the history of medicine his passion.)

Ruth Lang
1ˢᵗ March 1906 – 11ᵗʰ March 1995

W e have come here to say prayers for a wonderful lady who left us for all time last Saturday.

Although she had lived in Cambridge with Charles and Brendel and the children for only the last eight years or so, those of us acquainted with her felt we had known her for a lifetime. We knew her as Mrs Lang senior, or as Grandma, but in fact her real name was Ruth – a name rich in associations in Jewish history. Those of you who did not know her closely would be interested to know that she studied Physics at University College London in the 1920s – probably the first woman student in the faculty, and then went on to gain a PhD degree on work in Photo-elasticity. She must have enjoyed her student days and coped happily with her position as a young woman within an environment of boisterous young men. She was very fond of telling us how, one day, her car disappeared and [she] found that the young men students had lifted it bodily up the stairs and plonked it in front of the entrance hall. Needless to say, they helped her to get it down again. Because of her commitment to physics and science in general she met her future husband, who was one of the pioneer founders of the Physics Society and later of the Institute of Physics. So although I never knew him personally, I knew that there was a Mr Lang involved in Physics. What we did not know at that time, long before she came to Cambridge, was that there was (as it were behind the scenes) a Mrs Lang similarly involved.

Ruth Lang was a marvellous person, always busy, always cheerful, always occupied. She was skilled in wood carving and silver work and enjoyed it, and I am happy to have one of her carvings, which she gave me on my 80ᵗʰ birthday. She liked going shopping if there was something needed in the house and relished the challenge of getting to the shops on her own legs until a couple of years ago. She liked to be involved. Hanna and I recall many occasions when we were invited to a meal with the Langs, when we would always find Ruth helping in the kitchen as part of the family.

I suppose the things about Ruth that Hanna and I, and I guess many of you here, recall about her was her strong sense of independence, which she combined with a warm personality, her attachment to Judaism and her dedication to her family. Her family here were supportive in an *exemplary* way, but she too was supportive of them... I am sure that her love and example live on in her children and grandchildren – not least in her lovely Cambridge granddaughters.

Yehi zichrona livracha
[May her memory be for a blessing.]

In Memoriam: David Tabor

October 23rd 1913 – November 26th 2005

Funeral address delivered by Michael Tabor on November 30th 2005

F irst, let me thank you all for being here today. On behalf of Hanna, Daniel, Hazel and myself I would like to thank you for the love and friendship you have shown to David and Hanna over the years; and for the many acts of kindness performed by many of you for David and Hanna over this last and difficult phase of David's life.

Almost exactly a year ago I came over from my home in America to help clear out my parents' flat in Westberry Court. One of my tasks was to sort through David's personal papers. I am sure many of you here have had a similar experience. I found, of course, many pieces of family memorabilia and history. Let me tell you about some of them.

The first relates to David's father who, in the late nineteenth century, served in the Imperial Russian Army as an armoury specialist and, somewhat unusually for a Jew, held the rank of a non-commissioned officer. He lost his job because of the official anti-Semitism of the time. However, I found a copy of a letter of recommendation, written over a hundred years ago, from his commanding officer to help him find a new job. That letter, in its way, marked the beginning of a long journey undertaken by my grandparents – a journey so typical of so many Jewish families of that dark, bygone era – that ultimately led them to England where David was born, in Notting Hill Gate, on October 23rd, 1913.

I found reports and certificates attesting to David's brilliance as a schoolboy and as a student at Imperial College; there were essays and articles that tell us of David's passionate commitment to, and leadership role in, the Zionist Youth movement of his day; there were letters arranging for him to travel to Australia to conduct war-time research; and letters offering him his first staff appointment, starting immediately after the war, at the Cavendish laboratory where he worked, with the greatest distinction, for the rest of his professional life. Most important of all, was a special telegram he sent home from Australia to his parents in 1943. As many of you will recall, on really important matters, David was often brief and to the point. This telegram read: 'Am in love and getting married'. That telegram marked the beginning of his sixty-two years of marriage to Hanna.

There was one other item that I found that I want to tell you about that dates back to David's days as a research student in Cambridge before the war. It was a plain postcard from the Cambridge Jewish Students Association, postmarked, if I recall correctly, Cambridge, 1937, and addressed to David's digs in Cambridge. The postcard read as follows: 'Dear Tabor, this Shabbat your portion will be – and a particular reading of the day was cited – and ended with 'Services will begin promptly at 8:30am'. The last sentence made me smile since my father didn't always relish early morning starts – especially on the weekends. However, this postcard tells us some very important things: that David has been associated with the Jewish community in Cambridge for the best part of seventy years – all his adult life in fact; and that even then, all those years ago, the community knew it could always count on him. That never changed.

I realize that as I am standing here – and I suspect that some of you are thinking the same thing – that for so many years, for so many decades, it was always David who would be standing in front of you as I am now. Perhaps officiating at a funeral for a friend or colleague and saying a few thoughtful and kindly words of tribute. On countless Shabbats, it would be David leading the morning service and – as I will always remember – reading the prayer for the Royal Family and for the State of Israel in his clear but gentle voice. On many a Yom Kippur it was David whom you asked to give the Kol Nidre address; and those that I remember were always thoughtful and mercifully brief. And, for some of you, on that happiest of occasions, it was David who helped prepare your sons and daughters for their Bar Mitzvahs and Bat Mitzvahs.

But what about David the man who we are remembering today? A man who, in my reckoning, combined wisdom and kindness to an unsurpassed degree. I could speak at length about his great professional achievements, and the many and substantial honours that were bestowed upon him and that he wore so lightly. I could tell you of his great professional integrity and natural diplomacy, his scholarship, his wisdom, his warmth, his kindness, his modesty, his humanity, his lovely smile, and his delightful sense of humour; and if I was as learned as my father I could perhaps illuminate his many attributes, and the great decency with which he led his long life, with quotes from the Talmudic sages that he knew so well and loved so much. But perhaps that is not really necessary - for in our hearts we all know who David was and what he stood for. So, like my father on those most important of occasions, let me brief.

I believe David epitomized all that is good and true about Judaism. To his wife Hanna he was a loving husband for sixty-two years. To his parents, now long gone, he was a devoted and dutiful son. To his brothers and sisters, Simon, Bessie, Alfred, John, Esther, and Henry, he was 'Dod' the beloved brother - the brother they could always count on, and the brother of whom they were forever proud. And to his children Daniel, Hazel, and myself, what can I say? You all know the answer: we could not have wished for a better father or more inspiring role model. And to all of you here today, who was David? I can only guess what you are feeling at this moment, but I believe that to all of you – to all of us – he was a dear and true friend. Today is a difficult day, but there is a plain and simple truth that will carry us through, for we all know that in our hearts and memories David will live on for ever.

Thank you all for being here today.

DAVID TABOR

BORN 23 OCTOBER 1913

כ"ב תשרי תרע"ג

DIED 26 NOVEMBER 2005

כ"ד מרחשון תשס"ז

A Wise and Scholarly Man

אי'ננבון וחכם כמוך

Dearly loved by all who knew him

ת'נ'צ'ב'ה

HANNA TABOR

BORN 30 APRIL 1923

י״ד א״יר תרפ״ג

DIED 20 AUGUST 2010

י׳ אלול תש״ע

A wise woman is a gift from God
(Proverbs 19:14)

ומה׳ אשה משׂכלת

Deeply missed by family and friends

ת״נ״צ״ב״ה

הכנסת ספר תורה
Dedication of the Sefer Torah
in memory of David Tabor
and to honour Hanna Tabor

Cambridge, 20 May 2007

Daniel Tabor

The scribe completing the Sefer Torah, in the house of the chaplain to Jewish students

The procession to the synagogue

The procession (Jesus Green)

The Sefer Torah is carried by Barry Landy, accompanied by the Chief Rabbi, Lord Sacks

*The procession in Thompson's Lane, approaching the
synagogue*

Daniel Tabor

The Sifrei Torah,' welcoming' the arrival of the new Sefer Torah to the synagogue

The Chief Rabbi, Lord Sacks, with the Sefer Torah

The Sefer Torah in the Ark

Acknowledgements

We are most grateful to Stefan Reif for writing the foreword to this book. Thanks are also due to Barry and Ros Landy for inserting the Hebrew, Aramaic and Yiddish phrases and extracts from David's manuscripts, and for helping with the preparation of the text; and to Sarah Schechter for translating the Russian phrases. Many thanks to Les Culank for supplying the photographs of the *matzevot* (gravestones), reproduced alongside the eulogies. We are grateful to the Royal Society for permission to use the photograph of David that appears on the cover. We are also grateful to the editor of the *CJRA (Cambridge Jewish Residents' Association) Newsletter* for permission to reproduce David's poem *Chaloymes,* the tributes to Charles Fox and Sir Nevill Mott, and the articles *The Rabbi and the Journalist,* and *Cambridge 1936-39.* Thanks are due to the Editor of *The Jewish Chronicle* for permission to include two of David's articles. We are most grateful to Ben Blaukopf and the late Gordon Squires for the photographs of the dedication of the Sefer Torah. We are also grateful to Margrette Marks for typing up most of the talks and addresses; and to Michael Tabor for typing up two-thirds of the Kol Nidre talks.

Daniel Tabor